UNDER PRESSURE

LIVING LIFE AND
AVOIDING DEATH ON
A NUCLEAR SUBMARINE

RICHARD HUMPHREYS

Names of Royal Navy personnel have
been changed to protect privacy.

Mudlark
An imprint of HarperCollins*Publishers*
1 London Bridge Street
London SE1 9GF

www.harpercollins.co.uk

HarperCollins*Publishers*
1st Floor, Watermarque Building, Ringsend Road
Dublin 4, Ireland

First published by Mudlark 2019
This paperback edition published 2021

13 5 7 9 10 8 6 4 2

Text © Richard Humphreys 2019
Illustrations © Tom Hughes 2019

Photographs courtesy of the author with the following exceptions:
p 44 POA Phot Gary Davies/MOD; pp 59, 132 Wood/Express/
Getty Images; pp 66, 103 Navy News/Imperial War Museum;
p 136 Associated Newspapers/Shutterstock

Richard Humphreys asserts the moral right to
be identified as the author of this work.

A catalogue record of this book is
available from the British Library.

ISBN 978-0-00-831307-4

Printed and bound in Great Britain by
CPI Group (UK) Ltd, Croydon

MIX
Paper from
responsible sources
FSC™ C007454

For my father, who loved life
V.J.C.H.
1928–2016

'Submariners themselves were regarded as not quite the thing – smelt a bit, behaved not too well, drank too much. They were regarded as a sort of dirty habit in tins.'

Admiral Sir John Forster 'Sandy' Woodward,
One Hundred Days, 1992

CONTENTS

AUTHOR'S NOTE

I switched off the radio, made my way slowly up the stairs, shut the bathroom door and shed a tear. It was 16 November 2017, the day after the Argentinian submarine the ARA *San Juan* went missing in the South Atlantic off the coast of Argentina. At first, in those early days, it was unclear what had provoked the accident or what fate had befallen the crew, whether they might somehow still be alive beneath the waves. But then, with time, the cause of the tragedy became clear. An electrical malfunction had short-circuited the battery, which led to a complete loss of power for the old diesel-powered submarine. The *San Juan* had then sunk to the ocean depths, before finally imploding under the intense water pressure. The entire crew of 44, which included the first female submarine officer in the Argentine Navy, Eliana Krawczyk, had perished.

On hearing of the crew's horrible fate, my thoughts switched back to my own period of service aboard a submarine and how blessed I'd been not to have suffered a similar fate. There are innumerable fine lines between life and death when operating in one of the most testing environments the world has to offer, where one wrong move can almost instantly bring chaos and disaster. After the *San Juan* tragedy, friends who had previously never seemed the slightest bit interested in my naval career started pumping me vigorously with questions about submarines, the dangers involved in underwater living, and exactly how I retained my sanity during the long weeks and months away at sea, cut off from the rest of the world. This book is a direct result of those conversations.

At the age of 18, in the mid-1980s, I became a member of an elite group who served aboard Britain's nuclear deterrent, continuing my service for the following five years, while the Cold War was still hot and nuclear confrontation seemed scarily imaginable. In the 30 years since I left the Navy, submarine living and operating have remained fundamentally the same, although the creature comforts – including email, laptops, PlayStations and other products of the digital age – mean that some aspects are possibly easier now than they were during our stand-off with the Soviet Union.

I hope that what you are about to read will go a little way towards explaining the raw, real-life experience of what it's like to spend prolonged periods of time on a submarine. I've tried not to focus on the military aspects, although by necessity some of these will come into the story, but have rather concentrated on how it feels to live day-to-day in this claustrophobic, man-made environment, describing the pressures it exerts on both one's mind and body.

This is a book about life lived at the extremes, and there are few more extreme situations than living underwater in what is effectively a giant, elongated – if beautifully stream-lined – steel tin can. I hope that it informs, shocks, excites and entertains, and that it moves you, the reader, to spare a thought for the brave men and women who at any given moment are patrolling the world's waters, keeping their silent vigils.

The ID card issued to me on joining HMS *Resolution*.
I'm going for a Mick Jones from the Clash vibe.

DIAGRAM OF POLARIS SUBMARINE

AMS 2, including CO_2 scrubbers, electrolysers, COH_2 burners, freon removal plants and diesel generators

Motor room, including main propulsion motor, aft escape tower and main shaft clutch

Reactor compartment

Propeller

Rudder and afterplanes

Engine room, including main turbines, main gearing and chilled water plant

AMS 3, including manoeuvring room, motor generators, auxiliary motors and turbo generators

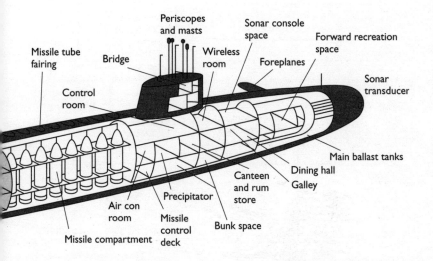

Missile tube fairing

Control room

Bridge

Periscopes and masts

Wireless room

Sonar console space

Foreplanes

Forward recreation space

Sonar transducer

Main ballast tanks

Dining hall

Galley

Canteen and rum store

Bunk space

Precipitator

Missile control deck

Air con room

Missile compartment

POLARIS SUBMARINE HIERARCHY

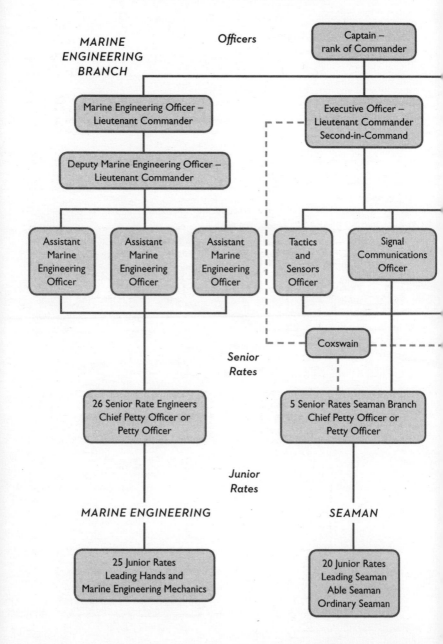

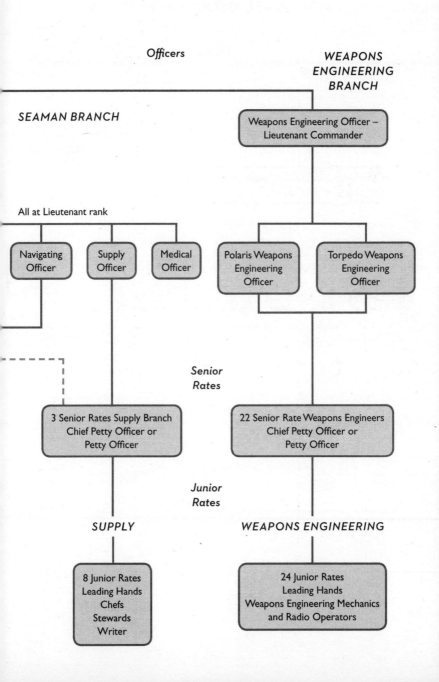

Officers

WEAPONS
ENGINEERING
BRANCH

SEAMAN BRANCH

Weapons Engineering Officer –
Lieutenant Commander

All at Lieutenant rank

Navigating
Officer

Supply
Officer

Medical
Officer

Polaris Weapons
Engineering
Officer

Torpedo Weapons
Engineering
Officer

Senior
Rates

3 Senior Rates Supply Branch
Chief Petty Officer or
Petty Officer

22 Senior Rate Weapons Engineers
Chief Petty Officer or
Petty Officer

Junior
Rates

SUPPLY

WEAPONS ENGINEERING

8 Junior Rates
Leading Hands
Chefs
Stewards
Writer

24 Junior Rates
Leading Hands
Weapons Engineering Mechanics
and Radio Operators

GLOSSARY

Terminology

alongside: status of submarine when berthed at jetty, in *Resolution*'s case at Faslane, awaiting to go to sea for patrol or work-up. Also where ship maintenance, storing ship, and loading both missiles and torpedoes – at Coulport – take place.

AMS (auxiliary machinery space): three areas on the submarine – AMS 1, 2 and 3 – where various bits of machinery are located.

angles and dangles: deep-water procedure where submarine dives and heads back to surface at steep inclines to test if boat is safely stowed for sea. Any noise generated by falling pots, pans or bits of machinery could give boat's position away on patrol. Great fun.

ARL (Admiralty Research Laboratory) table: located aft and on starboard side of control room. Mostly used when surfaced. Map lies on top of it and periscope navigational fixes taken from landmarks are applied to chart to calculate submarine's position in conjunction with SINS.

attack team: warfare team under guidance of XO reporting to captain, who has overall command. Consists of sonar team, tactical systems team, warfare seaman officers, XO and captain.

auxiliary vent-and-blow system: back-up vent-and-blow system in case of failure of main systems. May be used for diving and surfacing of submarine.

bathythermograph: instrument to measure changes in water temperature at different depths. Also used to measure velocity of sound in water. Sensors located in top of fin and keel.

BRN mast: supplies submarine with instantaneous navigation information to lock down its latitude and longitude at PD.

bubble: 'up bubble' means bow of submarine is angled up; 'down bubble', bow angled down; 'zero bubble', boat kept steady on depth. Controlled by afterplanesman.

casing: outer non-watertight upper hull of submarine, designed for hydrodynamic performance. Pressure hull is the inner hull.

CEP (contact evaluation plot): time-bearing plot constantly in operation on patrol where every sonar contact is plotted so its course, range and speed can be calculated for firing solution or to avoid collision.

control room: centre of operations, where captain commands submarine and planesmen manoeuvre, surface, dive, and go to and from PD using ship control console. Houses attack and search periscopes, attack team fire-control and plotting systems. Systems console located here, which controls ballast and trim pumps, hover pump and periscopes. Slop, drain and sewage tank is blown here and hydraulic system monitored.

Coulport (Royal Navy Armament Depot Coulport): on Loch Long, Scotland. Military facility that stores and loads Britain's nuclear weapons carried by submarines, first Polaris, then Trident.

1 Deck: nav centre, control room, wireless office, sound room, sonar console space, electronic warfare (EW) shack containing radar room, electrical equipment space with closed room containing navigator's maps.

2 Deck: entertainment and living spaces: wardroom and officers' bunks, senior rates' mess and annex, upper bunk space, coxswain's office, sick bay, galley, scullery, junior rates' dining area and mess in upper level of torpedo compartment.

3 Deck: senior and junior rates' bunks, junior rates' toilets, laundry, AMS 1, missile control centre.

dolphins: gold submariners' qualification badge to denote fully qualified submariner, gained after passing on-board oral examination. Panel consists of XO, chief engineer and coxswain. Worn on upper-left chest.

EBS (emergency breathing system) mask: used in emergencies when fire causes poisonous smoke to billow through submarine. Plugged into various

couplets around submarine, known as built-in
breathing system, which supplies fresh supply of air.

emergency surface procedure: to avoid catastrophic fire,
flooding and sinking of boat, all watertight bulkhead
doors are shut, full ahead is selected on engine
telegraphs, emergency air supply is used to fill ballast
tanks with air, causing submarine to surface as quickly
as possible with planesmen controlling pitch.

Faslane (HMS *Neptune*): on Gare Loch, Scotland. One of
Royal Navy's three operating bases. Centre of naval
operations in Scotland and home of the nuclear missile-
carrying submarines, in my day Polaris, now Trident.

fire-control system: computerised system on submarines,
designed by Ferranti and Royal Navy, using series of
pre-set algorithms and other tactical information from
on-board time-bearing plots and sonar room to
calculate firing solutions for torpedoes to target and hit
enemy vessels.

flying the boat: phrase suggesting submarine has similar
moving characteristics to aircraft while dived, with
pitch and depth controlled by foreplanes and afterplanes
tilted either up or down to make submarine push
upwards to surface or dive towards deep. Amount of
angle on planes coupled with speed of boat determines
angle of descent or rise, just as an aircraft's lift by its
wings is determined by speed and angle of attack.

gash: collective name for all the rubbish on a submarine,
collected, crushed and fired out by gash gun into ocean.

goffa: non-alcoholic soft drink.

HMS *Dolphin* (Gosport): former shore-side centre for submarine training. Royal Navy Submarine School was relocated to HMS *Raleigh* (Torpoint) in 1998.

LOP (local operations plot): time-bearing plot using information from sound room or periscope to calculate target motion analysis on ship or submarine contacts.

PD (periscope depth): depth equal to length of periscope when dived.

Perisher: Submarine Command Course, so-called because candidates pass or perish. Run twice a year for *c.* 24 weeks, taking in simulation exercises shore-side and sea-going exercises on nuclear submarine. Success leads to second-in-command, then captaining nuclear submarine. Failure, a bottle of whisky and never again setting foot on submarine.

pipe: boatswain's call used by quartermaster to pipe aboard captain on change of crews and pipe exiting captain off boat. Also used for flag officers – rear admiral and above – if visiting boat.

Polaris: Britain's first submarine-based nuclear ballistic missile system, in service from 1968 to 1996, when the last *Resolution*-class submarine in service, HMS *Repulse*, was decommissioned.

reactor: nuclear reactor in reactor compartment powers submarine, generating heat that creates steam to provide power for turbines, which turns propeller, and

for all electrical equipment and machinery to maintain
life-support systems.

'Resolution' class: four nuclear ballistic missile
submarines (SSBN) built for Royal Navy as part of
Polaris programme, each armed with up to 16 UGM-27
Polaris A-3 nuclear missiles. The capital ships of the day,
named after surface ships with a glorious past:
Resolution, *Revenge*, *Repulse* and *Renown*.

scram: reactor shutdown to ensure core remains safe and
doesn't overheat, melting the boat.

scran: collective term for food, originally naval acronym
for sultanas, currants, raisins and nuts once given to
fight scurvy.

scrubbers: used to remove CO_2 from submarine so crew
don't die of asphyxiation.

SETT (submarine escape training tank): vast concrete
tower at HMS *Dolphin*, Gosport, where simulated
escapes take place.

SINS (ship's inertial navigation system): internal
navigation system, fitted with gyroscopes,
accelerometers and velocity meters, that constantly
updates submarine's position.

SSN (nuclear-powered attack submarine): nuclear
submarine not carrying nuclear weapons, known as
hunter-killers for ferocious pursuit of Soviet
submarines. HMS *Conqueror*, which sank the
Argentinian *General Belgrano*, was an SSN. They were
armed with torpedoes and anti-ship missiles.

SSBN (nuclear-powered ballistic missile-carrying submarine): see 'Resolution' class.

tactical systems team: part of warfare team, providing complete tactical picture for captain and XO using information from sonar via sound room and periscopes if at PD, through use of target motion analysis to calculate course, speed and range of any given contact.

thermocline: temperature differentials within body of water due to seasonal variation, local conditions or latitude and longitude that give submarines acoustic blanket to hide in from sonar.

Trident: current British nuclear missile system that began replacing Polaris in 1994.

warfare team: team responsible for fighting the submarine under leadership of XO, who in turn reports to captain.

work-up: sea trials in front of onboard teaching staff ensuring crew are capable of taking submarine on deterrent patrol.

wrecking team: engineering team looking after forward part of submarine and watch-keeping at systems console in control room.

Ranks and roles

AB (able seaman): Royal Navy rating in seaman branch, above ordinary seaman and below leading seaman.

afterplanesman: controls afterplanes at bow of submarine, tilting them back to surface, forward to dive. Also steers submarine to left (port) and right (starboard).

captain: commanding officer of submarine, also referred to as 'skipper', 'the man' or 'God'.

chief ops: chief petty officer in charge of sound room as well as sonar ratings and any other senior rates who are sonar specialists. A highly experienced sonar operator, usually excels at quizzes.

chief wrecker: chief engineer who operates and watch-keeps at systems console, leading a team of junior rate wreckers maintaining engineering systems at front end of boat.

coxswain: ship's senior rating, normally with rank of chief petty officer or warrant officer.

CPO (chief petty officer): senior non-commissioned officer in most navies, rank between petty officer and warrant officer.

foreplanesman: controls operation of foreplanes from the control room. Works in conjunction with afterplanesman to maintain correct pitch and depth of submarine, crucial when at PD.

junior rates: heartbeat of submarine, keeping her alive and buzzing every day. Responsible for storing ship, cleaning and scrubbing out for inspections, watchkeeping duties, and also for most of drinking and entertainment while at sea.

Lt Cdr (lieutenant commander): commissioned officer in Royal Navy, above a lieutenant and below a commander. Heads of departments on submarine were all lieutenant commanders, as was XO.

leading radio operator: leading hand working in wireless office monitoring signals from Command Centre at Northwood. Equivalent rank to corporal in Army.

leading seaman: either a sonar operator or tactical systems operative, a key member of attack team.

leading steward: personal steward to captain, also likely to do a turn on ship control steering submarine.

master-at-arms (MAA): *see* **coxswain.**

MEM (marine engineering mechanic): driving force on boat, ensuring all mechanical and life services from nuclear reactor to air purification and laundry tick over. Most importantly, keeps toilets flushing.

MEO (marine engineering officer): senior engineering officer tasked with safe working and operation of nuclear reactor and all other engineering systems. Reports to captain. Usually at rank of Lt Cdr. Mine was cerebral and friendly, and played a mean Spanish guitar.

NO (navigating officer): seaman officer in charge of navigation, holds charts and maps of patrol area in a locked room on 1 Deck. Member of warfare team. Reports to XO. At rank of lieutenant. Known as Vasco or pilot.

OOW (officer of the watch): seaman officer, captain's representative while watch-keeping at sea, preserving safety of submarine in all aspects, especially avoiding grounding and collision. Accountable to captain for safety of entire submarine while on watch.

QM (quartermaster): in charge of external security of submarine, managing ship's crew inventory so no one gets on board without his knowledge. Also helps with logistics of storing ship.

RPO (reactor panel operator): monitors reactor and associated electrical and propulsion systems from manoeuvring room.

senior rates: non-commissioned officers, either petty officers or chief petty officers.

surgeon lieutenant: doctor on board, hides in sick bay armed with paracetamol. Unlikely to display standard bedside manner. At rank of lieutenant. Also does turn at ship control on patrol.

TASO (tactics and sensors officer): seaman officer, part of warfare team. Reports to XO. At rank of lieutenant.

WEM (weapons engineering mechanic): junior rating looking after maintenance of torpedoes and electrical systems of sonar and other computer systems.

WEO (weapons engineering officer): in charge of loading, maintenance and firing of nuclear weapons and torpedoes. Reports to captain. Usually at rank of Lt Cdr.

XO (executive officer): the Jimmy, Number 1 or second-in-command of submarine. Like captain, will have passed Perisher course. Overall in charge of warfare team. Reports to captain. Usually at rank of Lt Cdr.

INTRODUCTION

The Cold War, deep under the North Atlantic. Probably, but who knows? I certainly don't. Right now we could be anywhere. All I can hear are whales communicating with each other, a haunting sound that's somewhat tragic in delivery, like a loved one bereft for eternity.

Theoretically, we are 15 minutes from the start of Armageddon. That's the time it would take between us receiving the firing signal from the prime minister and the nuclear warheads being launched. I'm on patrol – submarine patrol – aboard a sizeable chunk of Britain's nuclear deterrent. We are the hidden. We see and hear everything, but only ever listen – we never communicate. A highly trained, motivated, elite team of submariners, we're the best in the business. It's the middle of the night in the control room, all the dials bathed in soft red lighting. I haven't slept well for days; I've got bad skin and my body clock has gone haywire. And then it happens.

A distant noise. Panic sets in. Undetected by our sonar, it's as if the intruder has come from nowhere. The crew freeze, the next 30 seconds drip by … What is it, friend or foe? Have we been detected and compromised? Suddenly, the tell-tale sound of a submarine's propeller screams over the top of us no more than 50 feet away. All hell breaks loose. I literally dive full-length into a seat on the fire-control system, as we scramble around looking for answers. We assign the rogue sub a target number and track it as it passes to the stern of us, then, phantom-like, gradually fades away to the east, never to be heard from again.

That was close, way too close. The captain made the call – correctly, of course – that it was making far too much noise to have detected us. But even so, most of the crew on watch when it happened are now nervously fidgeting, thinking to themselves: *How did we miss it?* There's a lot resting on our – mostly very young – shoulders. We can never be detected or compromised. Nor can we seek and destroy. We can only evade. Our job is to hide the bomber, this monster of the deep.

*　　*　　*

HMS *Raleigh*, Torpoint, Cornwall, nine months earlier.

I'd had a plan – a clear plan – since joining the Royal Navy that I wanted to serve with the elite. I wanted to be challenged, and if I was going to do it I needed to throw my heart and soul into it. I also needed the adrenaline fix. As a restless but determined soul who wanted to do something a tad different with my life I decided on the Submarine Service, the 'Silent Service'. I wanted some of that, and although I had no idea what it would entail or what was required both mentally and physically, it appealed as a test. I'd been intrigued by submarines since childhood and had regularly seen them at the Plymouth naval base on our family's annual summer break to the beautiful South Hams region of Devon. We'd spend at least one day visiting Plymouth Hoe for a game of crazy golf followed by fish and chips, gazing out to sea where, among others, Drake had sailed in 1588 to engage the Spanish Armada. Plymouth had been a vital centre during the Age of Empire, and all the sailor-scientists had set sail from here – Cook, Bligh and Darwin. Its naval history carried on and on through the two world wars, right up to the fleet of vessels I'd see on my boyhood holidays.

After lunch the family would take a guided trip round the warships on one of the boats that departed from the Mayflower Steps on the seafront, and we'd work our way past the might of the modern Navy. The moored-up, rusting warships seemed large, robust, even a tad soulless.

Meanwhile, the submarines tied up alongside looked anything but; sleek and powerful, with a large helping of intimidation to boot, they radiated a sense of mystery and glamour. I'd sit there looking at them, marvelling at what lethal pieces of machinery and wondrous feats of modern engineering they were. Enigmas to me in many ways: one minute powering forward on the surface like a ship, then in a flash simply vanishing under the water, wholly hidden from the world, completely self-sufficient, relying on no one, asking for nothing.

Unbeknown to me at the time, on these holiday boat trips I was witness to the changing nature of the Navy. It was no longer the surface boats that dominated the dockyards but the submarine. For where once it had been the battleship, aircraft carrier and frigate, now it was the age of underwater supremacy.

But even at that age I did sense that perhaps the ultimate mental examination was – as it still is – coping with life under the sea. A world without natural light, cooped up alongside more than 140 other men, eating the same food, breathing the same air, surviving together in some of the most forbidding conditions imaginable. Before I was to attempt this, however, at the age of 17 I tried to join the French Foreign Legion in Aubagne, near Marseilles. I'd ventured out there alone by ferry and train – having told my mum and dad I was off inter-railing with a couple of mates – and passed all the initial tests, both fitness and written, only to be told by a corporal of the 2nd Foreign Parachute Regiment that I needed parental permission as I was not yet 18. This was never going to happen. Immaculately dressed in fatigues and green beret, the chiselled Englishman cheerfully advised me to reapply in a few months, seemingly implying it would be a mere formality and that a career in the Legion lay ahead. To this day my mother knows nothing about this episode in my life, nor does my father.

I'd been fortunate enough to win a scholarship to public school in the Midlands for some of my secondary education. I didn't come from a wealthy family – my family had grafted all their lives – so boarding school had certainly been an eye-opener as to how the other half lived, but it was useful in developing coping measures and survival instincts, and enabled me to get along with pretty much everyone. It was here that I first read Simon Murray's *Legionnaire*, his classic account of serving in the Foreign Legion and the very book that had inspired my ill-judged trip to Marseilles. But the book also taught me something else – that the traditional trip through further education and then college or university wasn't for me. I'd had enough of textbooks, teachers and essays; it was time to do something against the grain for a few years and see where I ended up.

There didn't seem much point hanging around in the real world, as Mrs Thatcher and her Conservative government were wantonly destroying the West Midlands and most of northern Britain. The very recent miners' strike was evidence of that, with the hitherto unseen spectacle of the British police having pitched battles with miners in desolate fields across South Yorkshire. It seemed that tradition and heritage no longer stood for anything. The miners, who could trace their family lineage back to the start of the Industrial Revolution, when the mining industry supplied power to steam engines, generated electricity and heated buildings, now found themselves on the sharp end of the politics of hate and the systematic destruction of the industrial heartlands. Glasgow, Newcastle, Manchester, Liverpool, Leeds, Sheffield and Birmingham were the major cities on the brink of economic collapse, and this had a knock-on effect on their satellite communities, my hometown of Wolverhampton being one.

Wolverhampton had gained its fortune on the back of the wool industry in the Middle Ages, when it flourished as a small market town. Its prosperity continued through Tudor Britain, and its first canal opened in the early 1770s, stimulating economic and industrial growth through the transportation of raw materials and goods. During the 19th century, at the advent of the Industrial Revolution, Wolverhampton boomed as a centre for steelmaking, coal mining and lock-making, and most of the country's cables and anchors were made there at the height of the British Empire. It was also in the 19th century that the town and the surrounding area picked up its nickname of the 'Black Country', when the soil was turned black with soot deposited by all this burgeoning industry.

The railways reached Wolverhampton in 1837 and, coupled with the canal system, further increased the accessibility of the town; indeed, the Great Western Railway soon became a major employer in the area when it opened a locomotive repair factory in 1859, a large bicycle manufacturing industry further enhanced economic prosperity, and by the time a public park was opened, quickly followed by an art gallery, library and hospital, the town was thriving as it headed into the new age.

The early and middle part of the 20th century had been kind to the town, and its football team – along with Manchester United's 'Busby Babes' – were the best in the land. Captained by legendary centre-half Billy Wright, Wolverhampton Wanderers won three league championships in the 1950s and an FA Cup at the end of the decade, making them the unofficial world club champions.

But the mid- to late-1960s saw a painful decline in both Wolverhampton's – and the industrial western heartland's – economic fortunes, and by the mid-1970s a third of the population lived in council housing, with unemployment rising and immigration causing deep divisions in the West Midlands.

Enoch Powell, author of the infamous 'Rivers of Blood' speech, was the local MP for Wolverhampton South West. I'll never forget as a very young boy answering the door to him while he was on the stump in the first general election campaign of 1974. I remember opening the door to the palest-looking man I'd ever seen, his skin like alabaster, head slightly tilted forward. He stared at me intensely with fixed, unblinking eyes.

'Mum and Dad are up the road at the neighbours,' I told him bashfully.

I may have been very young but I knew immediately who he was – I'd seen him on the TV – but of course I didn't know about the general furore he'd caused in the country as a whole. At this point my elder brother Chris joined me for moral support, so Powell doffed his trilby hat, wished us good luck and walked off at a gallop to Number 6.

Wolverhampton in the 1970s staggered along with rising unemployment and seemed to me to possess an underlying threat of violence. The place was suffering – economic death by a thousand cuts – and by the time the Tories came to power in 1979, hell-bent on changing the social and economic outlook of the once-great industrial heartlands of the Black Country, most of northern Britain was finished; the collapse of the industrial working class and the north–south divide of Thatcherism had well and truly begun.

As a six- and seven-year-old, I'd watch the news of factories shutting, car plants closing, the oil crisis and the first miners' strikes. Even at that age I was aware that this wasn't business as usual, but it didn't give me sleepless nights. I was too busy with my newfound love of sport. Whether it was football, rugby or cricket, it all came fairly easy to me, and I guess that sport was also an enjoyable release from overly zealous, annoying teachers. Football was my obsession; morning, noon and evening I'd be out in our road, in the park, or driving my parents mad, hammering the ball against the garage door. Slightly introverted and on the shy side, I was wary of people until I got to know them, and was not much of a conversationalist. Instead, I lost myself in sport and my other passion – music.

Later on I captained the school football team and played for the area and district teams. Football was my life. Aged 14, I was lucky enough to have trials with my hometown club, Wolverhampton Wanderers. I'd been training in their youth set-up and had been on a couple of tours with them, including a memorable trip down to London where we played the borough of Hackney, coincidentally my home for the past 16 years. We had stones and bricks thrown at us from the touchline, and the match was suddenly called off after 30 minutes.

I didn't make the grade for Wolves. I remember the coach coming round to my house, sitting me down in front of my mum to break the upsetting news. It hit me hard, the first time I'd failed at something.

But my childhood was happy for the most part, except for losing both my maternal grandparents at the end of the decade, my grandfather dying six months to the day after his wife; married at 18, they'd been together for over half a century before both bowing out at three score years and ten. I was particularly close to my cousin Stephen. Four years older than me, he was cool, played the guitar and was into New Romantic bands, particularly David Sylvian and his group Japan. I didn't see him as much as I'd have liked, and by the time he reached 18 I'm sure he didn't want to be seen hanging round with this spotty 14-year-old with braces.

It was the hot summer of 1982 and the World Cup on the telly when the phone rang. Dad answered. It was a friend of my Uncle Brian, telling him that Stephen had been found dead in his car. In shock, we assumed he'd been in a car crash, but in fact he'd had a massive heart attack and a friend had discovered him slumped over the steering wheel with the horn blaring. Dead, and not yet out of his teens. The post-mortem revealed he had an enlarged heart muscle. I was devastated by his death, but of course I had to be as strong as I could for my aunt and uncle. I didn't know how to process my feelings or communicate my grief, so I just bottled it up and allowed it to fester. It wasn't really an era for discussing feelings – that wasn't how things worked – and my whole family suffered in silence.

My parents would let me out of the house for hours at a time. I'd disappear up the local park, playing football, climbing trees, annoying the neighbours, staying out till dark; fish and chips every Saturday lunchtime, going to Woolworths to buy The Jam's *Sound Affects*, my first LP – not 'vinyl', it was never called that, a modern term used by people who were never there in the first place; playing 'knock and run' … slowly I was tapping into a new sense of adventure as my body and confidence grew.

As I became older, this love of adventure – plus Simon Murray's book, which had provoked my failed attempt to join the Legion – pushed me towards a life away from formal education. When I returned from Marseilles, the Navy looked like the next best option for an unconventional life – and I'd also heard that the Submarine Service paid well. Serving Queen and country never entered into it for me, as I was neither nationalistic nor a particular fan of the monarchy. The only people who ever talked about fighting for Queen and country were – and still are – feckless politicians who'd never done, nor ever would do, any of the fighting. Queen and country? One was outdated as an institution, the other past it as an idea. No, I wanted to do it for me.

1

BEASTING

HMS *Raleigh* is a naval establishment on the banks of the River Tamar in Cornwall, where all new recruits commence their Part 1* training. At the height of a warm and bristling English summer in early July 1985, while the country was looking forward to Live Aid from Wembley and Philadelphia, all I had in front of me was 11 weeks of utter hell and lunacy. I arrived on the Torpoint ferry from Plymouth, trying to give off an air of nonchalant irreverence. I decided I'd try to get on with everyone and make the best of it, and attempt not to get too downhearted if things didn't go according to plan. I was nervous, yes, but I had to exude some positivity if I was to make the grade.

My grand intentions were destroyed within 24 hours. We were put together in a class of around 25 recruits and given a lecture of induction by the master-at-arms. He told us he was to be addressed as 'Master', pointed out who the senior

---

* Naval training is split into three parts: Part 1 is basic training; Part 2 is shore-side specialist training; Part 3 is at-sea training.

NCO (non-commissioned officer) on the staff was, and then, much to my amusement, had us pledge allegiance to the monarch and sign various forms with next-of-kin details. I was then given a service number and whisked to the barbers for a brutal No.1 haircut – the only option – for which I had to pay £1.20. Piss-take. Next, once I'd climbed into a smelly sweater used by every training recruit, I had my photo taken for my naval ID card with said new haircut. I was then measured by the stores staff, hats were shoved on and off my head, shoes and boots tried on, more sweaters hurled at me, with tape measures poked into my every nook and crevice. Finally, once I was handed a kit bag, I walked over to my dormitory – a 'mess deck' in naval terminology – ready for the long slog to begin.

I soon got chatting to my fellow squad members, who seemed like a good bunch, a nice mix of cocky, hard-working and methodical types. I reckoned I'd be OK. I was assigned a bunk, and told that lights-out was at 22.00 hours and we'd be woken up at 5.30 every morning. Shitsville.

Just before I drifted off for my first night's sleep I distinctly remember wondering what the hell I was doing there and thinking that there had to be easier first rungs on the job ladder. The next thing I knew it was 5.30 sharp, the lights flicked on, to the accompanying shout of 'Hands off cocks, hands on socks!' That morning – like every other that followed – started with half an hour spent scraping away at my mostly whiskerless face with an old cut-throat razor, then a shower and a further 30 minutes making my bed, which had to be done to perfection: sheets, counterpane and blankets all folded in a variety of ways, snug and neatly presented or my bedding would be launched straight out the window.

Our instructor was Chief Petty Officer Jenkins, a Cornishman who had served most of his career on carriers as a radar operator. He was a softly spoken man of the sea whose bark was worse than his bite, and he used the word 'boning' a lot. At first I thought he must have been a butcher in a previous life, but it soon became clear he was talking about the opposite sex – he could have given Roy Chubby Brown a run for his money. And then one day Jenkins vanished from our course and wasn't seen again. I never discovered what happened – maybe the Navy found out he was a sexual deviant and had him put in rehab or a strait-jacket. He was replaced by another officer, CPO Williams, on what was to be his last posting before he retired. Supportive and occasionally encouraging, he was confident enough to let other training departments do the shouting.

Basic military training is pretty consistent across the armed forces: 11 weeks of 'militarisation' to instil a sense of discipline, teamwork and organisation, with a focus on weapons training, firefighting, swimming and damage control. You've got to be fit, as there are obstacle courses, long runs and gym sessions, including gymnastics and rope-climbing. Although I absolutely hated gymnastics, the one sport I'd been hopeless at while at school, being quite unable to reverse-somersault over the pommel-horse, I was brilliant at rope-climbing; I could get up a rope in around six to seven seconds, which took some doing.

Part of our training involved a trip to Dartmoor, a long weekend in the middle of nowhere with a compass, food and tent, trying to get to various rendezvous points within a certain amount of time. As ever when I ventured outdoors, the heavens opened with monsoonal fury, and we spent most of the weekend soaking wet, cold and hungry. One guy got pneumonia and ended up in hospital for a month. Most of the weekend, John – probably my closest mate in the squad – and I kept seeing what we believed were shadowy figures, which flicked in and out of our peripheral vision. Everyone thought we were going loopy through lack of sleep and hunger, hallucinating even. We were later told that members of the SAS had been shadowing our movements all weekend for training purposes.

I soon picked up the fundamentals of life in the Navy, including ceremonial duties and basic drill – yes, lots of drill, far too much. I still don't know why there was so much of it. Its purpose was to instil pride and discipline in the group, but I never saw the point. It seemed a relic of a bygone age, resonant of empire and the need to keep the plebs in place. Getting screamed at by a gunnery warrant officer was a particular favourite, especially when there was close eye-to-eye contact; no matter what I or the rest of the squad did, it was important to keep a straight face as the guy's blood vessels reached bursting point with the rounds of expletives he hurled in our direction. Partly detached from the whole experience, I was usually overcome by the smell of Kouros emanating from his every pore.

Other than advanced seamanship, firefighting, navigation and basic weapons training – comprising pistol shooting, self-loading rifle (SLR) and general-purpose machine gun (GPMG), which consisted of hitting a stationary target from 25 yards with a machine gun firing God knows how many rounds a minute – the one element of basic training I remember was this pointless shouting and hollering by the instructing staff, which often bordered on bullying and abuse. I could deal with the insults and swearing ('You fucking spunk bubble!' being my personal favourite), along with the questioning of my manhood and parentage, but I wondered how this would improve me as a person and sailor? To me, the idea that abuse is good for the individual and team ethic, and that subordinates – even in a military environment – should be taught through fear and humiliation, is just wrong. All it served to accomplish with me was strengthening my sense of self, while making the training staff appear like wild-eyed testosterone monsters. Why an experienced NCO would squander all the knowledge he'd toiled for over a long and successful career by hurling inane obscenities at a group of young men, and in some cases boys, I never understood.

I'm not sure what the Navy is like nowadays, but in my day it verged on the nonsensical. I'd spent time at boarding school, where the bullying was at least as bad as you got in the armed forces, so I'd dealt with this kind of treatment before. I knew you had to let it wash over you and not engage with the teaching staff. If you did, they'd exploit each and every one of your weaknesses, and devote themselves to making your life a misery.

I used to be up for hours every evening, washing and ironing; it felt more like a dry cleaner's than military training. And the ironing was ridiculous – creases here, creases there, creases fucking everywhere, creases sharp enough to cut a loaf of bread. I'd spend an eternity perfecting the use of the steam cycle, and if I was required to wear ceremonial dress the next day I might as well forget about getting any sleep. Polishing shoes was another major ball-ache – up all hours, using a naked flame to heat the polish, then applying it with cotton wool, then, Bob's your father's brother, shoes so gleaming you could use their reflection to shave in. Again, I'm not sure how all this was preparing me for a career under the waves, but hey-ho, that's basic military training; you are scum, the lowest of the low, a number. Nothing more, nothing less.

The extreme demands made on us were a shock to many. Some of my group had suffered enough by the end of Week 5, as their bedding and locker were launched out of the window onto the parade square for the umpteenth time, their kit and shoes deemed insufficiently clean. Their punishment? Cleaning the toilets with a toothbrush. Utter sadism. After 11 gruelling weeks I passed the course, and Mum and Dad came to see me pass out. There was an official video made of the day, and as the camera panned around the parade square before the arrival of the First Sea Lord, the VIP for the day, it caught my parents arguing intensely about the workings of the new camera they'd bought for the occasion. I presume they got it working in the end as I still have a couple of photos that I've shown my

Summer 1985 and I'm passing out. Proud as punch in my full Royal Navy guard uniform, armed with a self-loading rifle, shoulders back, chest out, begging my father to get the camera working.

children, who never believed I actually went to sea or indeed was ever in the Royal Navy at all.

What did I learn from basic military training? Not much, to be honest. Everyone talked about it being good for developing team skills, but I wasn't so sure. It seemed more like 11 weeks of self-preservation by any means. I learnt how to iron and I became an expert shoe-shiner. If all else failed I could keep my kit nice and neat; 'Humphreys kept a good locker' would be a fitting summary of my time there.

The most rewarding aspect of basic training was that I was taught how to sail at sea. I spent a long weekend on Plymouth Sound on a boat learning the basic skills of seamanship and how not to endanger myself or other crew-members. I loved it so much that in the time between my leaving submarine school and joining the Polaris fleet – some three to four weeks – I used to sail two retired admirals from Portsmouth round to Southampton, a distance of about 12 miles, where they'd lunch at the yacht club while I'd get a fry-up at the local café. They'd talk about the scourge of communism, Labour leader Neil Kinnock being a Russian spy, and bringing back the death penalty and the birch as I sailed them home to Gosport. They'd head off to their houses and I'd pootle around the boat, have a gin and a smoke, then return to base. Heady days.

The aim of Part 2 of the Navy training course at HMS *Dolphin*, in Gosport, was to instil the highest standards of professionalism demanded by the Submarine Service. I travelled from Plymouth across to the Navy's other major historical port city, Portsmouth. From here it was a hop on a ferry over to Gosport, the home of HMS *Dolphin* and indeed the Submarine Service since 1904. Dominating the skyline was the submarine escape tank. It sent shivers down my spine just thinking about how I'd cope with that infamous aspect of the training. I was also required to demonstrate an intimate understanding of the different engineering, weapon and safety systems that run the submarine and keep the crew safe.

This seemed a long way away from cleaning toilet bowls with a toothbrush, ironing shirts and buffing shoes. Fortunately, the days of kit musters, long runs and drill were long gone. It was classroom-based, head down in books-type learning, absorbing the basic principles of nuclear and diesel propulsion. There were various exams after each stage: hydraulic systems, auxiliary vent and blow, electrical systems, the workings of a nuclear reactor, torpedoes and ballistic missiles, CO_2 absorption units, the different ventilation states on board, the workings of the periscopes, navigational systems, electronic warfare, and radio and sonar systems – quite enough to fry your brain. This was followed by radar training, which I struggled with; it was all blips and blobs to me, a predetermined mess on a screen. I'm still very much in awe of air-traffic controllers and how they manage flights in and out of the major airports and monitor the sky.

HMS *Dolphin* was the very first time I saw serving submariners. The base was home to the 1st Submarine Squadron and the 'Oberon' class submarines, or O-boats, as they were called; these were diesel-electric submarines, Cold War intelligence gatherers also used for Special Ops drops and pick-ups (usually members of the SBS – the Special Boat Service – doing reconnaissance or covert landings). I'd mosey on down to the jetty and gaze at these sleek, stylish boats with their bulbous front ends where the sonar was mounted, wondering: *How do people live on something so small for weeks on end?* Sometimes I'd wait until the crew appeared, to get a glimpse at what this way of life might do to me. They always looked rough and greasy, with a deathly pallor about them. Doubtless they stank as well, although I never got close enough to tell.

These men were a throwback to the submariner heroes of the past, a tightly knit crew in their own secret world, all members of the exclusive underwater club, with the golden dolphins badge* to prove it. They may have looked gaunt and unkempt, but it was the swagger of their gait that gave the game way, confident but not cocky, men completely at one with themselves and their crewmates. It seemed like a lot to live up to.

HMS *Dolphin* was very much like going back to school, punctuated by the odd pint or six in Gosport, or over the water in Pompey town centre, in the footsteps of Admiral Nelson himself. One of the nightclubs, I think it was Joanna's, was a favourite haunt, treading through sticky,

---

* The dolphins badge is awarded to fully qualified submariners after Part 3 sea training and an oral exam.

beer-slicked carpets onto the dancefloor, dancing to Barry White, Marvin Gaye, Paul Hardcastle and Madonna, with one-night stands a-plenty – the dirtier the better.

The accommodation at the base was four to a largish room. There were no kit inspections, no hassle from the staff, a complete change from the horrors of Part 1 basic training. It wasn't without its moments, though. In the room next door a trainee submariner from Aberdeen scared us to death one night, returning back to base well and truly hammered, waving a gun around and threatening to shoot someone. We became scared very quickly, and amid all the screaming and panic I found him with his back to me. I gave him a hefty kick behind his right kneecap and he collapsed like an old block of flats being demolished, straight down in a big heap. As he hit the floor the gun flew out of his hand, and we pinned him down until security arrived and took him off to the detention quarters. Just like CPO Jenkins, he was never seen again.

The final stage of submarine training ended with four pressurised ascents of the 100-foot submarine escape water training tank (SETT), the enormous concrete tower that dominates the skyline on the Gosport side of the Solent as you leave Portsmouth Harbour. All the training had been leading to this point, for this was the test, the ultimate trial of nerve. This section of submarine training in the tank had seen a few deaths over the years, and put the fear of God into every young submariner courageous or stupid enough to attempt it.

Before I started, I had to sit in a decompression chamber that sits near to the tank itself to make sure my ears could endure the pressure I'd shortly experience in 100 feet of water. Then I was bundled into the chamber with around half a dozen other terrified souls and we waited for pressurisation to commence.

No one had told me about the hissing sounds as the air rushed in. I sat there holding my nose, clearing my ears and looking like a startled child, praying that we'd get to the prescribed depth pronto. The air temperature increased and I started feeling exceedingly wary of where this was going. Soon enough we reached the required depth of 100 feet and the air temperature equalised. The instructor announced, after what seemed an eternity of five minutes, that he would slowly release the pressure and that the temperature might drop. We finally returned to normal pressure at sea level and I clambered out disorientated, nauseous and nervous; 'shitting conkers' is the expression that comes to mind. Next stop, the tank.

I had to make two free ascents from 30 feet below, one from 60 feet and then, to my horror, an ascent from 100 feet, in a fully pressurised suit out of a cramped, claustrophobic escape-hatch based on the type you'd find aboard a real submarine. My nerves were shot to pieces as I clambered into the first side chamber, contemplating my first free ascent from 30 feet. There were around 20 of us sitting in the chamber, which was about to simulate a rushed escape from a stricken submarine. Trying to listen to the final instructions from members of the teaching staff, my mind wandered back to my childhood in the old Victorian central swimming baths in Wolverhampton; I'd be wearing arm-bands and a rubber ring, being pulled along on a rope by an unimpressed swimming teacher with my father looking on in hideous embarrassment, until he'd up and leave to wait in the car, unable to stand the sight of his limp-bodied son. I can't say I blamed him. Back then I was scared to death of the water, and if someone had told me I would be free-ascending from the murky depths a decade later, my seven-year-old self would have cried uncontrollably and probably pissed himself.

First off, the 30-foot ascent. The water started to rush into the chamber and I tried to clear my ears as the internal pressure equalised with the external water pressure in the tank (around 15 pounds per square inch) at 30 feet. Dressed in swimming briefs, lifejacket, goggles and nose plug, I was in the middle of the queue to get out. Very soon it would be my turn, and my heart was racing. I couldn't hear anything with all the noise of the water pouring into the chamber. Quickly, in what felt like seconds, the chamber was flooded, with just a small gap at the top left in which to breathe. Once the pressure equalised, the main hatch to the escape tank would open and it would be time to get it done. I was next in line at the entrance, taking a big, deep breath as one of the instructors pushed me under and out into the vast expanse of the tank. I barely had time to take in the surroundings as I was met by two instructors who seemed to take an eternity to let go of me. I glanced around, they released me and I started the ascent. I knew I had to breathe out all the way up, because the volume of air in your lungs increases as the pressure decreases, and if you held your breath, your lungs would simply burst. I pushed the air out and looked straight ahead as I glided upwards for what seemed like a lifetime before I hit the surface.

Next up came another big test – the free ascent from 60 feet, something that filled me with abject terror. Maintaining exhalation from that depth seemed to me a close call, but the instructor informed me that if I ran out of puff, and if I felt like I couldn't breathe out anymore, then I needn't worry – I should just keep blowing, as I'd still have 25 per cent of my lung capacity left. Of course, I didn't believe him. Water pressure increases the lower you go; at a depth of 60 feet, I'd be experiencing 30 pounds per square inch of pressure on my body. In addition, the greater the pressure, the greater the chance of a burst eardrum while equalising to the pressure in the tank. All of this information turned me into a nervous wreck as the water began to enter the chamber in preparation for the mock escape. I cleared my ears, and then I was next. 'Take a good, deep breath,' someone bellowed at me as I ducked down and pushed out into the tank. Within seconds a barrel-chested, slightly pot-bellied instructor appeared from a diving bell in the tank to make sure I was breathing out correctly. Meanwhile, in my head I was screaming: *Shit, let go of me before I run out of puff and my lungs give way!*

Slowly I started to rise, but this time I was really struggling to breathe out – the natural bodily response is of course to hold your breath. I got halfway up and a second instructor who'd been hiding in another diving bell came out to meet me and jabbed his outstretched hand into my rib cage to make sure I was exhaling. I clocked the depth gauges as I ascended, and I realised how deep this actually was. I had to regulate the blow, as I felt I was running out of capacity, but eventually I breached the surface, relieved I'd made it through unscathed.

The final part of these two days of hell was an ascent from 100 feet, with a simulated evacuation from a replica submarine escape tower. This involved climbing into a tiny compartment beneath the 100-foot tower in a hooded pressure suit. I clambered in, having only half-listened to the instructor, overcome by an adrenaline rush and heart palpitations. I couldn't yet vote, I was about the age at which I could learn to drive, yet it felt like I was putting my life in completely unnecessary danger, as if I'd sleepwalked into this nightmare in the hands of total strangers. The tower closed shut behind me and I was stuck in a minuscule space that was about to be flooded. I guessed that they were checking for signs of claustrophobia and stress, and I saw there was an implement for me to start banging on the pipes with if I couldn't hack it. Pleasant thought.

I climbed gingerly into the escape hatch, head to toe in a self-contained submarine escape suit; I knew I needed to plug myself into an air pipe that would inflate it as the water came in, making it fully pressurised. Suddenly it was time, and the water started to shoot in, my stress levels becoming almost unbearable as I was squashed into this tower, the suit inflating around me. As the water pushed against me, I tried to clear the pressure from my ears with the help of a nose plug, all the while trying to remember what I'd been told. I recalled all the stories of what could go wrong; at the very least I was expecting my eardrums to burst.

The pressure on my suit was immense now, around 50 pounds per square inch, and bubbles blurred my vision as

At once terrifying and exhilarating – a trainee breaks the surface after successfully completing the 100-foot ascent.

water rapidly filled the tank. I was terrified beyond comprehension, but within 30 seconds the hatch suddenly opened. After floating out I said my name and RN ID number to the instructor, who had gone to the bottom of the tower to meet me in a diving bell. I was then attached to a pole and shot up the 100 feet of water in around ten seconds. As I was now in a fully inflatable suit I remembered to breathe normally, in, out, in, out, reminding myself constantly that my ascent needed to be smooth, and that I should breathe all the way to the top. I suddenly popped to the surface, almost fully breaching out of the water, then floated onto my back doing a fair impression of the Michelin man, before I was finally led to the side of the pool and handed over to the medical staff for a once-over.

This was both the high point and the most nerve-wracking part of initial submarine training. The Navy stopped all pressurised escapes in 2009 and worked on a simulation basis instead. This seems like a shame to me as it takes away the key element of danger. Although I found it a suitably terrifying experience at the time, which I'm sure pales into insignificance compared with a real-life submarine escape, the retirement of the tank-ascents programme strikes me as an example of modern-day health and safety gone mad. It's worth noting that in 1987 on board HMS *Otus* in Norway,*

---

* 'HMS' can mean both 'Her Majesty's Ship' and 'Her Majesty's Submarine', with the context usually giving a clue as to which is meant. Here it's clearly a submarine.

two staff members from the SETT team escaped in pressurised suits from a depth very close to 600 feet, a truly remarkable achievement by an extraordinary group of men.

I was told shortly after my final examinations that, subject to vetting, I would be drafted to the 10th Submarine Squadron, which meant only one thing: nuclear deterrence. The 10th Submarine Squadron took their name from the heroic 10th Submarine Flotilla, who performed miracles in the Second World War in their defence of Malta from German forces, by keeping the country in supplies, as well as sinking German ships destined for Rommel and his troops in North Africa. In total the flotilla sank around 412,000 tonnes of Axis shipping. At the forefront of this effort was Lieutenant Commander M. D. Wanklyn, who torpedoed, sank or disabled around 127,000 tonnes of shipping, an astonishing feat that earned him the Victoria Cross and Distinguished Service Order (DSO). He was declared missing in action in 1942, aged just 30.

2

HMS *NEPTUNE*, FASLANE

It was time to head north to Scotland. Far from being an alien land to me, this was where my mother and father had moved for Dad's last job before retirement, to a small village called Houston, just outside Paisley, near the wonderful city of Glasgow. Dad then worked in Govan. I was going further north-west to Gare Loch, a sea loch in Argyll and Bute, about 25 miles from Glasgow. The loch, around six miles long and on average about a mile wide, is not at all what you might associate with potential Armageddon, as it's mostly a very peaceful place, almost suburban in much of its appearance, flanked by the picturesque, affluent seaside town of Helensburgh, with its polished Edwardian and Victorian houses dominating the skyline of the eastern shore. The village of Rosneath lies on the western shore, among blue-green hills, and it's at this point that Gare Loch narrows to just 600 metres wide, at what's known as the Rhu Narrows, after the tiny village of the same name. Here, at its southern end, Gare Loch joins the Firth of Clyde, providing access through the North

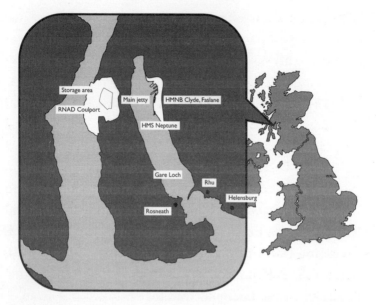

Channel to the main submarine patrolling areas of the North Atlantic.

It was further north on the eastern shore that the dominating fixture of the landscape lay in wait for this somewhat nervous-looking, anxious 18-year-old 'man'. The Clyde Submarine Base, Faslane, had been the home of the British nuclear deterrent since 1968, and was the Royal Navy's main presence in Scotland. Known as HMS *Neptune*, I was struck by its razor-wire security fences, the MOD policeman patrolling the perimeter fencing armed to the teeth, and the Comacchio Group of the Royal Marines doing hand-brake turns in their RIBs* as they raced up and down Gare Loch,

* Rigid inflatable boats.

keeping at bay any unwanted trespassers from the Faslane Peace Camp, a permanent CND (Campaign for Nuclear Disarmament) site since 1982.

The base had the usual accommodation blocks, parade squares, offices and training centres, as well as a hospital and massive canteen, but the whole place was geared towards the main jetty and the submarine that was harboured there: HMS *Resolution*, my new companion, a weapon of war capable of destruction on a scale hitherto unseen in any modern conflict. Its nuclear weapons could deliver massive explosive force, more firepower than all the bombs dropped during the Second World War, including the atomic bombs that destroyed Hiroshima and Nagasaki. For someone as young as me, this was hard to comprehend. Until that point I'd barrelled through life with a carefree attitude and a cheery sense of bonhomie; now I was about go to work on this most lethal of killing machines.

Before joining *Resolution* I was security vetted to within an inch of my life by a bespectacled, ruddy-faced man in a double-breasted pinstripe suit in a small office somewhere in HMS *Dolphin*. The office was well lit and looked particularly unforgiving as I entered: two chairs, his across from mine, two plastic cups and a notepad on my side laid out on a plain white table. Initially I heard footsteps in the distance – sharp, unforgiving strides as the man's steel-tipped shoes announced his imminent arrival from some distance away, reminding me of Lee Marvin in *Point Blank*. *Am I going to be on the receiving end of those?* I wondered. He entered the room, we shook hands and he proceeded to inform me that he was a vetting officer. *Vetting officer, my arse.* He was a member of the security services based in London, and it was his job to make sure I was of sound temperament and had no skeletons in my closet that would make it impossible for me to serve on the nuclear deterrent.

He asked a wide variety of questions, some about politics, others about family, starting with, 'Are you a communist?'

'*Nyet*,' I answered in Russian.

That went down well.

More questions followed, about my sexual orientation, whether I liked a flutter on the horses, and whether I could keep secrets about operations and the submarine. Then the Irish wing of my family – my mum's side – who hailed from the Catholic south, found themselves in his crosshairs. The Troubles were still in full swing – bombs, murder and misery across the water in the six counties – and he asked if I had any Republican sympathies. I replied that the notion of a united Ireland was a noble idea to aspire to, but the way it was being played out on the streets by lunatics on each side was ridiculous.

I detested the way the Irish had been treated by the British, the casual racism that they suffered, particularly after the Birmingham pub bombings; the endless Paddy jokes about how thick they were, told most nights on television by misogynistic, racist comedians. My grandfather was from Dublin. Crossing the water to find work decades earlier, he had grafted all his life and settled in the Midlands. I'm sure he must have witnessed this racism first-hand, but he never made comment about it. I relayed all this to the vetting man, who looked at me open-mouthed and speechless.

Then the final subject surfaced – nuclear weapons – and a series of questions designed to assess whether I was sufficiently sound of mind to be trusted to work in close quarters with a weapon that could wipe out a sizeable chunk of humanity. I, of course, kept *schtum*, too frightened to speak in case I said the wrong thing. All things considered, it was a topic best not to have too firm an opinion on and I hadn't really given it much thought until that point, there in that spartan room with a complete stranger sitting in front of me. All I knew about nuclear war came from nonsensical 1970s public information films. I didn't want my career to be over before it had even started, but presented with the scenario that at the age of 18 I might be party to delivering the most lethal weapon system in the history of warfare and play a role in the destruction of nameless millions was a little off-putting, to put it mildly.

'Are you comfortable with the use of nuclear weapons?' he asked directly.

'Yes,' I eventually answered.

The vetting man looked me up and down, then jotted some final notes in his folder. A week or so later I was informed I'd been positively vetted to serve my country. My national security clearance was Top Secret.

I presume fledgling submariners would have seen their careers end with a wrong answer. I know for a fact that some officers who had passed Perisher, the notorious Submarine Command Course,* and who had subsequently been offered the captaincy of a Polaris submarine, had declined, as they couldn't live with the awesome responsibility of having to fire their missiles in retaliation for a Soviet first strike.

Upon arrival at HMS *Neptune* I was met by two humourless MOD policemen, who proceeded to process my ID card for the base. Radiating machismo, they made it obvious that they were both armed – some sort of machine guns, by the looks of them – but I put it down to them not getting out much. It took more than an hour for them to register that a) I was indeed a human being and b) a new member of the ship's company. On reflection, they probably needed the guns, as they looked so out of shape they wouldn't have been able to chase down an intruder. I was led by these two charmers through three gates, all involving bag searches, then onto the jetty where I caught my first glimpse of HMS *Resolution*.

She lay there motionless, tied with ropes forward and aft, 80 per cent of her bulk hidden underwater. Sleek, black and athletic-looking, Britain's ultimate war machine had more than a hint of menace about her, as if she knew the punish-

---

* All captains have to pass the Perisher course to command a submarine, and all seconds-in-command on nuclear submarines will have also passed the course.

ment she could inflict, quite aware that she could disappear like a ghost and travel undetected for months, armed to the teeth with weapons of unimaginable destructive power.

Resolution was a Polaris submarine built by Vickers shipbuilders in Barrow-in-Furness to the south-west of the Lake District. The other three *Resolution*-class boats – submarines are never called ships, reflecting a time when submersibles were taken out to sea on the back of ships like boats – in the squadron were *Repulse*, *Revenge* and *Renown*, *Repulse* also being built by Vickers, the other two by Cammell Laird in Birkenhead. The Polaris programme was born of discussions between President Kennedy and Prime Minister Harold Macmillan that took place in the Bahamas in 1962, and became known as the Nassau Agreement. This ended the programme of airborne-launched nuclear missiles, which had been used by the Americans since the 1950s.

Britain had joined the trans-Atlantic programme in 1960 but had struggled to revamp the newer missiles to its existing squadron of Vulcan bombers, the beautifully designed delta-winged, high-altitude strategic planes that had been Britain's carrier of nuclear weapons since November 1953. With the withdrawal of airborne-launched ballistic missile systems, the plan was to switch to submarine-launched ballistic missiles, giving rise to the Polaris submarine programme. Britain would have their own submarines but would be supplied with American Polaris missiles. Building of the subs began in 1964, with *Resolution* being commissioned and finished in 1967, and completing her first patrol in 1968. Along with the other three subs comprising 10th Submarine Squadron's Polaris fleet, until its decommissioning and replacement by Trident beginning in October 1994, *Resolution* was the most powerful weapon of war ever built in this country.

With the advances in missile defence made by the Soviets in the 1970s, it was deemed that the existing Polaris warheads were vulnerable to interception around the major Soviet cities, particularly Moscow. The way around this was to develop a system whereby the missiles on re-entry would launch a multitude of decoys and counter-measures that would offer too many incomprehensible targets, thus overwhelming Soviet anti-ballistic missile defences while the real warheads slipped through. This became known as the Chevaline Warhead System, and had been kept in strict secrecy by successive Labour and Tory administrations. It was a wholly British design and represented a fundamental shift away from methods used in the American programme. By 1982, Britain, with this new warhead in place, had a fully independent deterrent missile system.

Longer than a football pitch, narrow and forbidding, HMS *Resolution* lay silent as death as I looked on – no machinery running, no sailors or stores being loaded on board, no hustle and bustle in the neighbouring support depots, just quiet and still. Even the Gare Loch was motionless – no birds or wildlife, only the tiniest swell lapping against her bow as if in reverence to this huge, black leviathan. She was a killing machine – everyone in this place knew it, most of all me. I was extremely nervous, almost a wreck by this point. On the jetty next to the submarine I exchanged forced pleasantries with the quartermaster (QM), the seaman in charge of the boat's security.

As he checked my name against the list of names permitted on board that day, I detected a Mancunian accent. I knew full well that if your name wasn't down, you weren't coming in. Had even the First Sea Lord – the highest ranking officer in the Navy – come a-calling unannounced and wasn't booked in for the day, he'd have had a long night waiting up top freezing his nuts off. Nothing was compromised at any point; clockwork and military precision were the order of the day as the security of the boat was paramount. My cockiness on passing Part 2 submarine training five weeks earlier had quickly dissipated, and it was with a deep sense of unease that I made my first steps across the gangway and prepared to go on board.

3

THE BOMBER

I was greeted on the casing by the coxswain, CPO Freddy Maynard, a gruff northerner of Yorkshire descent. On initial impression he seemed fair, despite possessing the look of a man not to be crossed in any shape or form. The coxswain is the chief of the boat, the head NCO who looks after its company in terms of discipline; if you're up before the captain because you got pissed in Helensburgh and started acting like a spoilt arsehole, it's the coxswain who'll be giving you the evil eye and enforcing any punishment according to Navy regulations. Chief of the boat, he's the third most important person on board after the captain and the XO.

It was time to go on board and see what all the fuss was about. Even though I'd had three months of training, this was the first time I'd ever stepped aboard a nuclear submarine. I was shitting it. The main access hatch was a straight drop down a ladder of about 10 to 12 feet, starting off vertical, then halfway down kicking out towards 1 Deck, as the top deck of the submarine's three decks was known.

The first thing I noticed was the claggy heat as I reached the bottom and turned 180° to carry on down to 3 Deck, where my locker and bunk were located. There was a distinctly stale odour down here: the ghosts of farts long dead, mixed with heat, oil and the CO_2 absorption-unit chemicals they used to recycle air back into oxygen. Add to that special cocktail the collective sweat of a crew of 143 men and bingo, you had the submarine smell. It was grim all right.

The second thing to strike me was what lay immediately above my head – and the need to duck. I cracked my forehead on the overhang of the steps down to 3 Deck, giving me a nice egg of a swelling above my left eyebrow. Although *Resolution* was the biggest submarine built by the Navy at that time, it was hellishly cramped in terms of living space, and moving around its tiny passageways required all manner of contortion. The *raison d'être* of the submarine is first and foremost machinery and functionality, with the bodily needs of men coming a distant second. I noticed valves, gauges, low ceilings, wires, switches and dials all round, and wondered how in hell I was going to cope learning the mechanics of all of this.

Two people couldn't pass on a corridor without one moving aside. You could stand in the middle of the passageways on 1, 2 and 3 Deck with your outstretched hands and touch either side of the sub. It was impossibly tight. Then there were the protruding pipes to bang your head on, bulkheads to trip through, small hatches to navigate, valves and dials all over the place, plus vertical ladders between decks

… there were risks everywhere. I had to pass through hatch after hatch and ladder after ladder before getting to my bunk at the bottom of the boat. The lack of space was giving me the fear. I couldn't let on, but on first impressions I wasn't sure life in a steel cigar-shaped tin can was going to work for me. It was all the equipment, for fuck's sake. It was everywhere you looked, coupled with those passageways and ladders eating up all available living space. Plus, there were nuclear weapons and a nuclear reactor to worry about, never mind their impact on the space. I was already starting to regret my ballsy decision to become a submariner.

The walls started to close in as panic got a hold of me, so I ran to the toilets to take some deep breaths. Christ, we hadn't even left the dock yet and I was getting into a state. I just needed to regroup a moment. Anyone who tells you they're not nervous when they first step on board a submarine is talking nonsense; the machinery, claustrophobia and alien smells, it's not good for the uninitiated.

Fortunately, the crew were mostly friendly and eager to help me settle in. I started to calm down after about five minutes as I messed about and put my kit in my locker along the passageway near my bunk space, although 'locker' is probably overdoing it. Was I really supposed to fit my kit for a two-month patrol in there? It was about half the size of one you'd find in a local swimming pool. There was a drawer back in my sleeping compartment where I could put my shoes and boots, but storage-wise that was it. I rolled out my Navy-issue green sleeping bag on my bunk and left my

Submariners hanging out in 9 Berth, where I spent my time in the land of nod. My bunk was the top one in the middle rack of three, never the bottom.

own pillow on top. The lack of privacy was plainly obvious. I was going to have to put my faith in the hands of my fellow crewmates and needed to be a good judge of character.

My main fear was that I couldn't do it, that it would all be too much. How would I cope? What dangers would lie ahead? How the hell was I going to remember everything – both my job and everyone else's – while contending with this ever-present claustrophobia. I'd only experienced being cramped in an escape hatch at the SETT at HMS *Dolphin*, but ten minutes in the submarine and I was already having a crisis of confidence. How would I manage being underwater without daylight for anything up to 80 or 90 days? And nuclear weapons? What if we had to use them?

It was still the height of the Cold War, with Gorbachev only recently having come to power, and the Soviets were hard at it. The Navy's hunter-killer nuclear subs tracked their aggressive submarines across the North Atlantic, in the waters between Greenland, Iceland, Scotland and the Arctic Ocean, while our diesel-electric O-boats penetrated Soviet waters via the Barents Sea. It was like time had stood still for the last 15 years, each side trying to gain the upper hand.

The Americans, too, in their 'Los Angeles' fast attack submarines, were playing cat-and-mouse games in the Pacific, with Reagan well into his second term as president and hawkish as ever, despite the apparent friendly overtures from the Soviets now that the affable Gorbachev wielded power.

I wasn't the only new starter; Philip, a bright, introverted lad from the Lake District whom I'd gone through training with at HMS *Dolphin*, was joining the boat at the same time. In addition, there were a couple of other junior rates,* all of us within the warfare team in the boat and collectively under the guidance of the coxswain.

As a submarine ship's company is notably smaller than, say, that of a frigate or aircraft carrier, the coxswain is the de facto master-at-arms, a person to keep on the right side of.

* 'Junior rates' is the collective term for seamen, able seamen and leading hands.

His main duties include being in charge of operating ship control while diving, surfacing and returning to and from periscope depth (PD); supervising the ratings who control the foreplanes and afterplanes, which regulate the depth and pitch of the boat; and overseeing new members of the crew. He would keep a steely eye on us throughout the forthcoming patrol.

The coxswain, like every other submariner on board, does more than one job. The leading steward, for example, will serve the captain his meals, then half an hour later will be on the foreplanes helping to bring the submarine to periscope depth. The beauty of this is that all qualified submariners can do their own jobs very well, but unlike other members of the armed forces they're also proficient at everyone else's. I might have been the nearest person to an emergency – be it fire, flood, hydraulic burst or ruptured air pipe – and I had to know how to deal with it and isolate the various systems involved in order to make the boat safe. This level of responsibility is unique within the services. Everyone here is in the same boat, and as JFK said, 'We all breathe the same air' – quite literally on a submarine, and for three months with no escape. You have to get along with each other.

In order to get to become a member of that rare club I had to undergo Part 3 training with a mentor at sea, and then an oral exam with the XO, the second-in-command, who himself had passed the Perisher course. Our XO had already captained a diesel submarine, so was biding his time until his own bomber command came through. The coxswain and usually one of the chief MEMs (marine engineering mechanics), comprised the remaining members of the exam board. All the knowledge I'd picked up at submarine school seemed worthless, for while it might help with my own job, it was of no use in terms of the many skills required to make the boat function, nor did it mentally prepare me to keep on top of everything. Everyone I met on board said the same: 'Forget all that shit, complete waste of time.' This was big-boy stuff, so it was time to knuckle down.

Resolution was 425 feet long by 33 feet wide and pulled a draught (distance from waterline to keel) of an inch over 30 feet. Her displacement when surfaced was 7,700 tonnes, and while diving 8,500 tonnes. The speed of the boat was roughly 20 knots surfaced and 25 knots submerged. The tear-shaped hull of a submarine is designed to be more aerodynamic when it is surrounded by water on all sides, hence it is faster underwater. The optimum depth to which the submarine can dive is over 750 feet.

As for her armaments: six Mk 24 Tigerfish torpedoes with a maximum range of 39 kilometres, travelling at a speed of around 35–40 knots, and 16 Polaris A-3 ballistic missiles with two Chevaline warheads per missile, with a staggering nuclear yield of about 225 kilotonnes in total. To put that into perspective, 'Little Boy', the Hiroshima bomb, yielded around 13–18 kilotonnes, while 'Fat Man', the Nagasaki bomb, weighed in at 20–22 kilotonnes. A deeply sobering thought when I considered what I was sleeping next to.

In terms of propulsion, the boat was fitted with a pressurised water nuclear reactor (PWR1) capable of powering it for a number of years. However, patrols were limited in duration by the supplies and food for the crew. Furthermore, the power generated by the PWR1 also helped with the distillation of sea water. Pumped into the two distillation plants, sea water was recycled into potable water by separating the salt vapour produced when it was boiled. The two plants could quite easily reach an output of over 10,000 gallons a day after which, free from impurities, the water made its way to the fresh-water tanks. The water was subsequently used mainly for cooling electronic equipment such as sonar computers and navigational equipment, but was also essential for use with reactor services, batteries and domestic services such as cooking. If any was left after all this we may have got some laundry done and had a 'shower'.

The nuclear reactor also created the electricity for the life-support systems on board, such as oxygen regeneration and the expulsion of unwanted gases like hydrogen, carbon dioxide and carbon monoxide, in addition to heating the air circulating round the boat and powering a number of other systems. The water deep under the world's oceans is around 3°C, so heat needed to be applied to various parts of the boat to keep the temperature regulated. Though not back aft in the engineering spaces or the galley, I might add, where temperatures could easily reach 40°C.

The reactor compartment was lead-lined, sealed and constantly monitored by the manoeuvring room engineers under the expert guidance of the nuclear chief of the watch, who in turn ultimately reported to the marine engineering officer (MEO), one of the most professionally qualified and important positions in the whole of the armed forces, period.

The submarine was split up into the different departments that made up the ship's company. These were headed up by the senior officers – the XO, weapons engineering officer (WEO) and MEO – who in turn reported to God himself: the captain. The warfare team was headed up by the XO, and its main function was to take the boat to war: tracking and evading enemy craft, keeping the submarine safe by controlling all the other systems on board, while maintaining the boat in a state of readiness to launch its devastating nuclear weapons.

The warfare team used the sound room, where you'd find the elite sonar team hidden in the dark, headphones on, as they collated and evaluated contacts through the use of passive sonar. Contacts were either audible sounds picked up by the sonar team, or, if a long, long way off, visible sonar traces were detected on one of their many screens and sent through to the control room, where they were tracked. Sound waves in the sea are affected by many things, the two main ones being the temperature and density of sea water, coupled with the many background noises of marine life and merchant ships. The sonar operator's job of accurately classifying contacts was a hellishly tricky one and required a great deal of experience.

Passive sonar is the non-active kind, meaning the sonar operator just listened and didn't actively transmit. He was able to identify the source of the noise by listening to the sound of the propellers, or using invaluable intelligence from SSNs,* which recorded the signatures of Soviet ships and submarines. The sonar operators were able to instantly classify the vast majority of sounds, be they a merchant vessel, oil tanker, fishing vessel or Soviet submarine. As passive sonar doesn't transmit sonically, its only major drawback is that it is extremely difficult to work out the range of a contact, as it's not getting a ping back from the target. Silence was paramount to evade detection, so active sonar was only ever used in sea-training exercises.

The data from the sound room detailing the craft's bearing and movement was then transferred to the control room, and from this information the tactical systems team (including myself) were able to work out firing solutions relating to the enemy's course, speed and range, which the XO and the captain could use or modify, depending on their own calculations.

The warfare team also navigated the submarine while she was on the surface, controlled the submarine at periscope depth for satellite navigational fixes and positioned the submarine before firing torpedoes.

The weapons engineering department were responsible

---

* Submarine submerged nuclears – known as 'hunter-killers' – were nuclear-powered submarines that didn't carry nuclear weapons.

The Royal Navy newspaper *Navy News* visited the submarine to celebrate 21 years of the deterrent patrols in 1989. Here's me posing for photos next to one of the torpedo tubes.

for maintaining and servicing the weapons on board, from nuclear missiles to the Tigerfish torpedoes, all of which were under the command of the WEO, who also pressed the trigger that would send the missile to its target. And yes, it *was* an actual trigger, coloured red just in case the WEO forgot what he was doing. In addition, they carried out electrical maintenance of the warfare team's attack systems, sonar, electronic warfare, radio transmission and navigation, to keep them functioning at all times. This could either be routine maintenance or a complete strip and rebuild, which involved a riot of electrical leads spread out all over the floor awaiting reassembly. 'Was it red first, *then* yellow?' I'd often heard them say. I still don't know the answer.

When the boat was on patrol, there was a separate team of electrical engineers who kept vigil over the nuclear missiles in a cordoned-off area in the missile compartment. As well as loading the missiles onto the boat at the armaments depot, they packed the conventional torpedoes at the forward end of the boat and maintained them throughout patrol in the lower end of the fore ends, or 'Bomb Shop' as it was known. The team was supplemented by radio operators who looked after all the communications coming from the Command Centre at Northwood in north London, and who were based in the wireless room.

The engineers ensured that the nuclear weapons and torpedoes were safe through a system of round-the-clock, fail-safe checks. Their thoroughness and knowledge were vital, for at any time before a patrol began the men from the ministry in the form of the NWI* team could arrive for a snap visit and ask some pretty awkward questions, under the auspices of a weapons inspection. This could result in the WEO or any member of his team being relieved of their duties. This actually happened on *Resolution*, where a WEO was removed due to a perceived lack of knowledge on the day. At the time, we thought his had been a strange appointment, as the individual concerned had come from a Special

---

* Nuclear weapons inspection.

Forces background and was thought to have been a serving member of the elite SBS. While that's great in its own right, it hardly qualified him for a life under the sea in charge of nuclear weapons.

The marine engineering branch, led by the MEO, were tasked with looking after the boat's propulsion, mechanical and life-support systems, and were split into two operating areas: aft (the back end of the submarine) and the control room, and everything forward of that. Aft of the missile compartment was their main focus, principally the manoeuvring room, for here were the controls that looked after the functioning of the reactor. Up to six people managed the detailed switches, pumps, hull valves and other bits of kit to make sure the reactor and its associated systems functioned correctly

The wrecking team manned the control room's systems console, where they assisted in diving and surfacing the submarine, raising and lowering the periscopes, and monitoring oil pressures. They were also responsible for the diesel back-ups and maintaining the battery, should we ever have needed to use it in the event of the reactor being shut down. As well as maintaining their favourite bit of kit, the garbage and sewage systems, they also ran the laundry on 3 Deck, where clothes tended to come back as smelly as when they went in.

The final department was the supply branch, whose sole function was to ensure the boat had all the necessary food, drink, toilet rolls (essential, obviously. I never fancied using

my hand to wipe my arse) and any other vital spares necessary for a ten-week patrol. This department was headed up
by the supply officer and staffed by chefs, who did a superb
job cooking three meals a day, plus snacks for months on
end in the most testing of working conditions. Next time
you're in a restaurant, take a good look at the kitchens and
all the chefs toiling in those cramped, hot and pressurised
environments. Now, while they might be able to go for a fag
break or some fresh air halfway through their shift, you
can't do that in a submarine. It's torturously hot and stifling
in the galley, with fire hazards aplenty … a total shit-show
where miracles daily occur in keeping a crew fed and
watered non-stop for three months, all of it happening in
around 15 square feet.

The supply branch was completed by the stewards, who
served the officers meals and drinks in the wardroom, and
then did a shift on ship control, driving the boat with its
changes of course and depth. And lastly there was the leading writer,* who could usually be found holed up in the
ship's office doing all the coxswain's admin; he also took his
turn at flying the boat as well.

Then there was the doctor, who occupied a small sick-bay
on 2 Deck, where he treated physically sick sailors. Don't
assume there were any mental health considerations, mind
you. If someone rocked up and complained, 'I'm not feeling

---

* The leading writer was responsible for helping with the HR function,
legal matters and other administration.

that great today, Doc. Can we have a chat about it, please?' the main gist of the doctor's response would be, 'Yes, of course, now fuck off.' He also doubled up doing a turn on ship control, where he helped look after the pitch and depth of the boat while it dived and was at periscope depth. The occasional failure to carry out that part of his obligations resulted in him being on the end of some almighty bollock-ings from the captain.

That said, these always seemed to wash over him, for he was not easily irked. I guess doctors don't get intimidated that easily. Although he was an officer with the rank of surgeon lieutenant, the doc I served all my patrols with preferred the company of the junior rates and drank heavily with us, always first in the queue for the pub on a night out and one of the last home, as well as being a heavy smoker. I'm not sure how he would have been judged by modern-day NHS standards, but he was great company – thoroughly entertaining, clever, level-headed and entirely unflappable. That said, I'm not sure I'd have wanted him taking my appendix out or resetting a broken bone.

The other major feature of the submarine particular to the nuclear deterrent was that it was made up of two crews, Port and Starboard (my crew). While one crew was out on patrol the other crew would be on the piss, on holiday or on training exercises. The main reason for this was maximising the amount of time any one of the four submarines could spend at sea. On these training exercises, we'd go to a simu-lated control room in Plymouth, where we'd practise both attacking and evasive manoeuvres in front of teaching staff who would judge our performance. It would be back-to-back, full-on attack-simulation training, with the warfare team under the leadership of the captain.

We liked these simulations. It made for a nice change to practise attacks on enemy ships or submarines, and they kept our hand in, for our main task on patrol was to evade and hide, not to engage or investigate like the SSN hunter-killers, or the diesel submarines that spent their patrols intelligence-gathering in Soviet waters and tracking enemy submarines. On the attack drills I usually found myself paired up with the captain as his periscope assistant. This consisted of helping the team effort by working out my own range of given target/targets using the angle of its bow and a 360° protractor slide-rule. The captain could then choose to ignore it, use it, or refer to it as a ballpark figure to help him with his own calculations. This full-on training lasted around a week, and to relieve the stresses of the day we partied hard in Plymouth. It led me back to some of my old 'run ashore' haunts on Union Street that I'd first encountered near the end of my basic training.

Aptly named, Boobs nightclub left little to the imagination; drink was consumed on an industrial scale, one-night stands were commonplace, with women and sailors in various states of undress while still in the club. Full-on debauchery ran amok, and I remember a particularly frantic half-hour of my own in the ladies' loos. The night would usually end side-stepping vomit or fighting men, occasionally women, or both at the same time, always alcohol-induced. Once, on exiting Boobs en route to our favoured Chinese takeaway, I saw a sailor come hurtling through the window; landing with panache, he dusted himself down and strolled off into the night like a gracefully listing galleon.

Our other haunt was Diamond Lil's, with Ronnie Potter. Ronnie played his Hammond organ while his wife sang mainly blue songs, as strippers did their thing on a raised stage, dragging inebriated sailors up for audience participation. All very bizarre, a kind of sleazy version of *The Good Old Days*, it was packed out every night. There was obviously no accounting for taste. The best hornpipe dance would win a free drink at the end of the night, but I'd never be in a sufficiently decent state to even attempt it. Although there were plenty of fights – mostly handbags – genuine violence was fairly thin on the ground among sailors. If there was any real trouble it tended to get started by the local thugs who wanted to put one over 'Jolly Jack' to prove that they still possessed the requisite manliness to survive in seaside cities they perceived as being 'invaded' by the Navy. All the recent debate about the disenfranchisement of the British working class is nothing new. I saw it first-hand in the mid-1980s on the streets of Plymouth and Portsmouth most Friday and Saturday nights.

4

ALONGSIDE

After simulation training ended, the Port crew returned from their patrol and it was now the Starboard crew's turn to take over the boat; resupplying it, carrying out any required maintenance and performing sea trials to ensure we were fit to go on patrol. The term 'alongside' refers to the period when the boat is stationed in port before it goes out on work-up and then patrol, and when routine maintenance and storing the ship take place. It's very much the calm before the storm, with the crew gradually moving from accommodation blocks in Faslane onto the boat. It doesn't happen all at once, so we don't get too cramped too soon.

I spent the days and weeks before my first patrol lugging food supplies on board and mostly avoiding the sharp tongue of the coxswain. It was pretty tedious, backbreaking work, and the other junior rates and I bitched about it constantly. But before my second patrol I was given the role of quartermaster, a hugely important job for a 19-year-old, particularly with the boat alongside. I was basically in charge of the external security of the submarine, making sure anyone coming onto the submarine had the correct pass, including members of the ship's company. Security was so tight that serving submariners from the 3rd Submarine Squadron – also based in Faslane – were not even allowed on the jetty where *Resolution* was docked. I checked visitor lists against who was expected, whether the captain had any guests arriving or if the MEO had any thespian types up from London. His wife had something to do with the theatre and so we'd receive visitors from time to time. And, since I would be the first person visiting dignitaries would meet on their arrival, it was important not to look like a sack of shit.

My favourite visitor was the Oscar-winning actor Sir John Mills, with whom I shared a pint down in the mess. He was immaculately dressed in a gold-buttoned navy blazer, shirt, cravat, grey slacks, pink Lacoste socks and brogues. We talked at length about the final scene in *Ice Cold in Alex*, which, he told me, needed quite a few takes. It's a classic scene in which Captain Anson, the character he played, takes a drink at a bar in Alexandria. The grand actor bemoaned to me that the director wanted to use ginger ale as a substitute for alcohol, but Mills thought it looked odd so they went with beer, and after about ten takes Mills was hammered and could barely deliver his lines. He had some experience of acting in submarine films set during the Second World War, and we talked about *Above Us the Waves* and *We Dive at Dawn*. I had developed an interest in acting when I'd played a few parts in school plays. I'd also seen a very young Kenneth

Branagh in the role of Henry V at Stratford, so I found this all fascinating. I still have a submarine photo signed by him somewhere. An extraordinary man.

Being QM enabled me to spend lots of time above water, overdosing on vital fresh air to top up my vitamin D levels before heading off to sea. It was a heavily pressurised job, and given the fact not only that CND supporters from the local peace camp had been threatening to board one of the Polaris boats, but that it was also the height of the Troubles in Northern Ireland and the base was high on the list of IRA bombing targets, I was slightly on edge.

The worst did in fact happen. In October 1988 three peace campaigners, fairly heroically it must be said, broke into the

Sir John Mills kindly autographed this picture of three of the four Polaris submarines, with HMS *Resolution* leading the way. The fourth boat would have been out on patrol.

Faslane base and onto a submarine. They cut through the outer wire, before scaling high-security fencing, evading Royal Marine patrols and the quartermaster – not me, thank fuck – and scrambling on board, making it all the way to the control room before capture. It wasn't *Resolution* that suffered this embarrassment but our sister ship, HMS *Repulse*. There was a huge amount of fallout of the conventional kind to deal with from the whole affair. Around ten personnel were reprimanded, including the commodore in charge of the base and the officer commanding the Royal Marines. You can bet your life the QM was also in the shit as well. The incident was covered up at the time, and apparently Mrs Thatcher blew her top when she found out. After that little episode, armed sentries were given the order to shoot on sight, but only as a last resort, in any future breaches of security.

There were two quartermasters on board, me and Charlie Stephens. Charlie was great, a rare character born in Salford and a Manchester United fan. Tough and firm, he liked a joke and was excellent at his job as a sonar operator. We lived in a small cabin at the top of the gangway on the jetty. It was a responsible job, but came at a price; I worked shift patterns, six hours on, six off. The 'graveyard watch' was from 2 to 8 a.m., which was never easy, and it was all I could do to stay awake. Sometimes I didn't, and I'd wake up frantically thinking I'd been asleep for three hours when it was probably only a couple of minutes. I'm not sure that would have gone down particularly well had anyone seen me.

Trying to pass those night hours in the cabin was horrendous – the radio would be on constantly, and since it was the days before rolling 24-hour news coverage, we were forced to endure some local radio station, or, if we remembered, we'd leave music tapes for each other to listen to. It was here I first discovered Tom Waits, with his deep, gravel-charged voice singing about the seedy underbelly of the US. He helped me to get through many a long night.

Crosswords were another antidote to the endless nights, but reading was a no-no as after 15 minutes I'd start nodding off, despite my best attempts to stay awake. Sometimes when I was off watch I'd go back to my room on the base to get some shut-eye. When in port, because of a lack of space in the boat, it made sense for the crew of a submarine to live at the base, but in the last few days before patrol everybody moved down to the boat, department by department.

We'd have a Royal Marine who would patrol up and down the jetty as well as other areas of the base. They'd be from Arbroath, where the Comacchio Group were based. They specialised in naval operations, like storming oil-rigs, which at the time were considered by the powers-that-be to be a prime target for terrorist attacks. Their other job, when not stationed in Northern Ireland, was the protection of the nuclear deterrent. They were decent guys to talk to, in many ways the 'thinking man's soldier'. I'd share my flask of coffee with them over a chinwag. One guy I recall who'd served in Northern Ireland told me about some of the serious scrapes he'd been in – and he'd obviously been deeply affected by it all. You'd call it PTSD now, but back then it wasn't thought to be anything serious, just something that had to be dealt with.

I'd do anything to make the time pass more quickly during those long nights: shadow boxing, press-ups, gabbling away like I was on speed to anyone who happened to be around – whatever it took to get through until morning. I'd also double-check the draught marks on the side of the submarine to make sure we weren't sinking while alongside. HMS *Artemis* sank in 30 feet of water in 1971 alongside at the submarine base in Gosport; her arse-end hatches had been exposed because of cable wires running through them while her diesel engines were being refuelled. Thankfully there was a very limited crew on board, and they were able to make it to the forward escape hatch and exit from the bottom of Haslar Creek to the surface half a day later to a hero's welcome.

I had a heater in the cabin, which helped during the winter months. I also wore the classic white submarine pullover to stave off the cold, and indeed anything I could add to keep warm. This didn't wash with some of the old CPOs, mind you, and I remember a certain nuclear chief of the watch grassing me up to the coxswain, since he didn't agree with the colour of the scarf I was wearing to fend off the icicles (I was an early exponent of Burberry). It was all right for him – he was around 20 stone, most likely pissed up, and encased in enough blubber to ward off the sharp end of a Scottish winter's night.

I used to spend hours just looking at this big, black messenger of death tied up alongside just yards away, marvelling at what an amazing piece of machinery it was; massive in size but minuscule compared with the oceans of the world that it pootled around in, unbeknown to the outside world. I often wondered, what if, what *if* we had to launch those missiles … would things ever get that bad? Although I cheered myself up with my belief that humanity would never attempt to self-delete and the missiles would forever sleep in their tubes, never to be roused, it was an unsettling thing to think of in the dead of night.

Being QM meant that if we had any visits pre-patrol from high-ranking officers, we would have to pipe the side (using a boatswain's call, or whistle for the layman) as they came on board or left. This always proved mildly amusing, as both Charlie and I were fairly hopeless at using the boatswain's call and the skipper would be glaring at us not to cock it up. Submariners are not really that great at old-fashioned cere-monial, and we tend to do things on the fly. We usually got away with it, even though our piping of the side left a lot to be desired, sounding like a strangled cat serenading the boss of the Submarine Service as he floated across the gangway. Admirals tend to float everywhere; they don't do walking.

Our other main ceremonial function was being the meet-and-greet if any important VIPs arrived for a pre-patrol 'look around'. It didn't get much more important than Queen Elizabeth, the Queen Mother. She arrived in a royal car, bulletproof, the works, and I was charged with opening her door, having been told not to do so until the car had come to a complete stop. I bowled up, pleased as punch, to what I thought was a parked car, looking a million dollars in my new pressed uniform, white gloves, belt and gaiters, gripped the handle and pulled, but it just kept moving forward at around 5 mph. The doors wouldn't unlock as the car was still in motion, so I found myself in the bizarre position of jogging alongside the Queen Mother for about 30 feet, looking in at her with an expression of horror on my face, my hand still glued to the handle. She stared straight ahead as if nothing had happened, obviously used to this sort of incompetence on a daily basis. I was embarrassed beyond words. She finally got out from the car with a simple 'Thank you,' while I burned with shame and stared straight at the ground.

When I finally looked up, the first person I made eye contact with was the coxswain, who was muttering something to me through clenched teeth. The royal visit was rounded off with the usual inspection of the ship's company, and the Queen Mother paid particular attention to one of our chefs, who reeked of booze from the night before and had a massive love bite on his neck. Clearly, she very much liked the cut of his jib as they chatted away, laughing and joking, and everybody else who was immaculately turned out in their dress uniforms and mirrored shoes never got a look-in.

The daytime was all hustle and bustle. I had to sort out the ship stores, as well as diving down to check the state of the propeller and the condition of the anechoic tiles below the waterline, whose purpose was to insulate against active sonar, radiating a distorted view back to any ship or submarine looking at the frequency waves. As well as blocking the enemy's ability to figure our true range, they also absorbed our submarine's noise, so passive sonar was unable to positively identify us. Yet another layer protected the pressure hull against sea corrosion, which could be potentially catastrophic, especially around sea-facing hull valves and periscopes; in fact, anywhere where the submarine was in direct contact with the sea. Sometimes, this layer would displace on patrol, so had to be fitted back on. Something similar was applied to the outer skin of space shuttles to reduce heat on re-entry. I shudder to think what each individual tile on a submarine cost the tax-payer, but these things were never discussed in the 1980s. It was simply buy, buy, buy whatever the Navy wanted, and *Resolution* and the other three Polaris boats were top of the tree in regards to defence spending.

5

WORK-UP

Before we were allowed to take the sub out on deterrent patrol, we had to go through a couple of weeks of sea trials called the 'work-up'. This was at-sea exercises to certify that we, the crew, were deemed sufficiently safe to take the boat out on patrol, and more importantly, trusted with carrying the nuclear deterrent under the oceans for up to three months. We would be put through our paces by 10th Submarine Squadron staff, who would take great pleasure in making our lives a complete misery. Humourless, and driven to the point of sadism, they had years of experience of serving on the deterrent, and they'd plan special exercises and drills to assess the professionalism of the crew.

These weeks never appealed to me, as they were basically an endurance test in trying to cope with sleep deprivation. I hated this as it would play havoc with my mind, moods, appetite, sleeping patterns, bowels … the works; it was the Grand Slam of mind fucks. The day would be spent doing 12 hours on watch (six on, six off, and repeat), dealing with simulated explosions, fighting mock fires, coping with casualties and various mechanical failures, either electronic or hydraulic, together with the dreaded reactor scrams,* performing dummy torpedo and missile drills – all underwater in a very enclosed space. It was also our turn to show other submarines and ships what we could do as we played out war games in the seas around the west coast of Scotland. I was being woken up every hour for another emergency, and by the end of it we were all thoroughly pissed off with the support staff – and they with us.

I remember being on watch in the control room when a thunderflash was set off about a metre from where I was standing, in order to simulate a collision. The noise was deafening, and I reeled away in complete shock, not knowing what was going on, caught totally unawares. I couldn't hear anything anybody was saying to me, having gone temporarily deaf while my body tried to regain some equilibrium. I slowly gathered my thoughts and senses, then proceeded to help my crewmates deal with the impending flood drill that followed. I complained to the staff member who'd lobbed the thunderflash next to me, but he just laughed. Cunt. I got him back some days later when I was running between decks with visibility low and an EBS† mask on; I gave him a tremendous kick up the arse and was gone before he could identify who it was.

---

* An emergency shutdown of the nuclear reactor.

† Emergency Breathing System. Looks like your run-of-the-mill gas mark as worn by the general military or a Tory politician.

In the six hours we were off shift, we would sleep crammed into the bunks, fully clothed with socks and shoes on; stinking, sweaty balls of stress awaiting the din of the next general alarm. Baaa, baaa, baaa. 'Fire, fire, fire! Fire in the deep-fat fryer!' You knew when one was due as the ventilation stopped just before, so we had a two-second head start. Ventilation was always turned off for emergencies, particularly fires, as feeding a fire with oxygen on a submarine leads to catastrophic spreading fairly rapidly. The exercises always seemed to take place just when I was going into a deep sleep, and I'd wake up a gibbering and usually dribbling mess.

With the ventilation off for what could be anything up to an hour, the air would get pretty hot and smelly, with condensation dripping off the pipes, so our clothes would be humming within a couple of hours. We would then catnap as long as we could until the next exercise. Doing six hours on and six off, the importance of sleep was paramount, as I'd have to go on watch at 2 a.m. for six hours, but I never felt like I could get back into a deep sleep while awaiting the next emergency exercise.

Work-up was probably the most intense period of the whole patrol cycle. We got through it because we were highly trained and could handle most of what was thrown at us, but at the time it seemed like a massive pain in the arse, and tempers could fly in an instant. Just the lack of sleep on its own was incredibly tough to deal with, especially at the beginning of my career, and while the absence of a regular sleep pattern was bad enough in itself, not having a planned sleeping routine made it ten times more difficult to cope. I'd be going on watch completely shattered, so doing even the basics felt like an enormous struggle. I always hoped we'd never have a real emergency during work-up, as most of the crew were like zombies by the half-way point.

I spent long periods of time in EBS masks, as in a real fire a submarine would very quickly fill with poisonous fumes spreading through the boat, the oxygen decreasing and toxins building up: ammonia, carbon monoxide and carbon dioxide, hydrogen chloride, nitrogen dioxide, sulphur dioxide and possibly hydrogen cyanide, to name but a few. The crew would have to plug their masks into the various air inlets around the boat. The problem was that once someone was plugged in, they were completely redundant in trying to fight the fire. This job then had to be taken on by firefighters wearing specialist breathing apparatus, who'd been trained in the highly tactical appliance of water. A submarine fire differs greatly to one in your average family home, where the fire brigade hose gallons and gallons onto the blaze. You couldn't do this on a nuclear submarine, as water sprayed around quickly led to electrical failure, shutting down the reactor, as well as the back-up diesel system, and causing a loss of power to the propulsion system, meaning that the boat would start going down rather than up. Permanently.

We had to get used to spending long periods in these masks, plugged into various emergency air outlets throughout the submarine to continue breathing. In addition, if you had to pass on some vital communication or order, you'd have to flit between the air outlets, holding your breath as you did. This could be fairly hairy at the best of times, especially when it was in the dark. On more than one occasion I was almost blue in the face as I raced down a couple of decks frantically searching for somewhere to plug myself in, squeezing past my crewmates occupying the air holes who looked at me like some sort of buffoon. But the comedy moment was trying to convey said communication or order to another member of the crew, a bit like trying to shout an instruction in a gale force wind. I used to try to act out various orders if no response was forthcoming, a sort of underwater version of charades. Crewmates loved it, but I'm not so sure about the grouchy teaching staff who'd be on board during work-up. I'd be met with a cold, hard stare: 'Not taking this seriously, son, are you?'

I was taking it deadly seriously, but there was always a place for making light of things, for having a sense of the absurd; it didn't mean I was any less committed than anyone else. I mean, how ridiculous, trying to pass potential life and death instructions via a mask. Complete nonsense. I made a point on future work-ups of always having a pencil and very small notebook to make notes in and pass on. Otherwise, the procedure took the bizarre form of me screaming at the top of my voice to a bewildered-looking crewmate, who would usually look at me with a glazed expression as if I were speaking Latin, although he'd occasionally head off gleefully as he'd understood the message.

The emergency procedures were exhausting both for us seaman types and the engineers who spent a lot of time crash-stopping and restarting machinery, mimicking reactor scrams, and simulating hydraulic failures and fires. The whole thing was a week of dread. Towards the end of the work-up we got the chance to pit our wits against some of the surface fleet as we were hunted around the west coast of Scotland, staging simulation attacks on frigates and destroyers. It was on these that the attack team honed all of the skills we'd learnt during the training weeks in Plymouth. The captain and XO would be in their element guiding this hulk of a boat through the busy waters as if they were nonchalantly manoeuvring a saloon car around a suburban roundabout. It amazed me how they were able to retain a full tactical picture of all the activity upon the surface, and it was a real pleasure to see them at work; periscopes being raised and lowered, ranges, courses and speed being worked out, ship control being bellowed at if the skipper couldn't see out of the periscope when we were too deep. Years of experience being TASOs or NOs (tactics and sensors officers or navigating officers) had culminated in them passing the Perisher course.

I remember us simulating the sinking of a frigate on a work-up exercise. We'd got within 1,000 yards at periscope depth undetected, 'fired' our torpedoes, gone deep to avoid counter-measures and escort attacks, then quickly surfaced next to her on our starboard side. It certainly got their crew's attention, *Resolution* hulking out of the water in close proximity to them. But for all the joking and bravado, work-up was a serious business, and submarines and their crew operated at a level of professionalism not seen in other branches of the Navy. We meant business – and everyone knew it.

The captain and XO's skills, honed over a decade or longer, were put into practice as we'd simulate torpedo attacks, the tubes flooded and a simulation water shot successfully fired on various frigates and destroyers without being detected. One skipper had a rather posh way of ordering 'Fire', with all the emphasis on the 'F', after which he just trailed off, as if he simply couldn't be bothered to complete the word; it was all I could do to keep a straight face. Being fortunate enough to serve under different captains gave me a close-up view of how they operated under pressure, and how they took the rest of the crew with them. Some were more vocal, others quieter with a steely determination, while a few were eccentric and possessed absolute faith in their ability to command. They were also being tested on work-up, and the teaching staff made their life as hard as anyone else's during that week of hell. Perisher lasts around four months, compared to a week of work-up sea trials, so I suppose this level of stress was a walk in the park for them.

The behaviour of the skipper in many ways was replicated by the rest of the crew. If he was aloof and distant, then you'd get some of the crew developing an 'us and them' attitude. But while it was fine for the captain to be remote, if you had junior officers walking around thinking this was an acceptable way to behave, they'd be in for a shock, smartish. Young officers just starting out on submarines were no different to anyone else, useless until they'd earned their dolphins. They were expected to put in the same graft as everyone, more so in some cases. Officers who got drafted to submarines from surface ships were usually the worst. Accustomed to much clearer reporting lines above the waves, it came as a shock to them when they were ignored by other crewmates whom they'd assumed would tell them where the various hull valves or other bits of the boat were. 'Go forth and multiply' was the standard reply. The rude ones would get special treatment, which could take various forms, the most brutal being someone pissing in their cup of tea when on patrol. Some captains were more rounded, approachable figures than others, the sort who understood the importance of inter-departmental relationships and were keen to maintain good morale within the submarine. A popular captain who interacted with the crew would always get more respect and hard work from them than one who was stand-offish.

During my very first work-up, Philip, the newbie with whom I'd gone through submarine training, suddenly threw a wobbly and tried to open the main access hatch at around 200 feet below the surface. He'd suddenly become claustro-phobic and his rational thinking mechanism deserted him. Poor soul, he must have been under such terrible mental strain to have attempted to open the hatch, and my heart went out to him. Leading up to the incident he'd showed no sign of being discombobulated. He simply flipped, just like that. He was physically restrained by some crew members in a needlessly excessive way – no half measures, they were taking no prisoners. I understand that his actions were alarming both for himself and for the rest of the crew, but why someone couldn't just have had a chat with him I'm not sure. Besides, did they really think he was going to open a hatch with around 90 psi of pressure bearing down on him? Of course, I wasn't a qualified submariner at that point, so I had to keep schtum, but it left a really bad taste in my mouth. I guess that's the military way. If in doubt, a bit of extreme violence will soon take care of it.

The submarine surfaced not long after, and Philip was airlifted off the sub in a helicopter and out of the Submarine Service for good. I never heard from or met him again. This sent me into a bit of a depression, as I'd known him very well from our time at HMS *Dolphin* and we'd been posted to the same submarine. My dismal mood paled into insignificance compared with what he himself must have been going through in the hours and days leading up to the incident. The overall consensus was that the boat had got rid of a wrong'un, and while I was aware we didn't want people who were unsuited to life under the waves, there were ways of dealing with them – and this wasn't one of them.

*   *   *

Being on board a submarine that's manoeuvred quickly and with gusto can feel in many ways like sitting in an aeroplane, albeit a plane with no windows. Towards the end of work-up and then once again before we dived on patrol, the boat was put through her paces by the captain to check if the foreplanes and afterplanes were working, and whether the submarine was stowed for sea correctly. While out on deterrent patrol it was essential that everything on board had been stowed away safely, because if we needed to move sharply away from a potential threat the last thing we wanted was for the pots and pans to start crashing around the galley. Angles and dangles – as the exercise was called – tested just this, with the boat darting into sharply angled descents and ascents to see what was or wasn't stowed properly. I used to like standing up and leaning with the angle – it was a magical sensation holding on, with plates and glasses flying, and tables and chairs careering around the messes.

There was one further exercise I looked forward to on work-up. That was when the aft planes and fore planes were 'jammed', so the sub would take on extreme bow-down or bow-up angles by an instigated loss of hydraulics. After flooding, this was next on the list in terms of catastrophic failure, for the submarine could be lost very quickly if the jam could not be righted – the boat would eventually pass its crush depth and simply implode. The aft planes and the fore planes at each end of the boat take care of controlling the depth when submerged, and also dive and surface the boat. When dived, the ship control team would instigate the exercise under the watchful eye of the captain. The planes would, one at a time, be put into a dive so you had the nuclear deterrent heading to the ocean depths either forwards or backwards. Reverse was by far the worse – imagine an aircraft coming in to land tail end first and you get the idea. The aft planes problem would usually be sorted out by going full hard astern, mid ships on the rudder and bow down on the planes to right ourselves. This was a fairly terrifying experience – going arse down at a 15° to 20° angle in an 8,500-tonne, 425-foot-long sub is not something I'd recommend. I used to hold on to the LOP (local operations plot) table as we dropped to the depths like a stone, smiling at my shipmates as if this were the norm. There was a finality about it, and it occasionally felt like this really could be the end; we'd only be saved by blowing the emergency air tanks and surfacing if the boat didn't right herself. Luckily engineering was always on our side and the boat would win out.

We would also dive the boat to test its pressure before it went on patrol. All hull valves or sea-connecting systems had to function at deep-diving depth. I used to like watching the Formica in the passageways bending the deeper we got, as did the toilet doors, which couldn't then be shut. I quickly learnt never to go for a shit in a submarine at 400 feet as I didn't fancy the audience. Meanwhile, the odd groan would issue from the pressure hull. There are two hulls on a submarine – the outer hull or casing is usually made of a lighter metal which forms the shape of the craft and has a deck built on the top so sailors can carry out their harbour duties, fish, do the hornpipe or store ship. The inner or pressure hull is made of solid steel; this takes the full force of the water pressure when dived. It's divided into sections that make up the submarine. These inner compartments are split into segments that are made even stronger by installing watertight bulkheads. *Resolution*'s hull was put together by assembling 15 different sections made on site in Barrow, then taken to the berth by a special transporter and welded together using specialist techniques and over 10,000 drawings as a guide. In the pre-digital age, this was a remarkable feat of engineering.

The deeper the dive, the more the pressure hull contracts to compensate. It must be able to cope with the outside pressures of water while maintaining a normal atmospheric pressure within the boat, so the crew do not start suffering any physiological problems due to a collapse in pressure. So, say you were at a depth of 500 feet, the hull would need to be able to deal with approximately 250 psi of pressure. If you tied some string across two points within the boat from port to starboard and monitored them as we dived, they would be tight when we first started our descent but the deeper you got to test the hardware and systems, the saggier the rope would become, due to the hull being compressed by the increased pressure of the sea outside.

The USS *Thresher*, the first nuclear submarine to be lost at sea, was carrying out similar manoeuvres after a major refit in April 1963. It was meant to be the fastest and deadliest nuclear submarine of its day, and having performed some angles and dangles it then started a deep-dive procedure. During this exercise, there was an electrical failure of the water coolant system, which catalysed an automatic shutdown of the nuclear reactor, and the boat was left plummeting arse-end first to the ocean floor without any propulsion, killing all 129 crew and shipyard personnel who were still on board. Various calculations that were carried out estimated that the sub broke up at around 2,400 feet, an abominable way to go, with the crew's final moments spent hurtling towards the seabed wracked with fear and despair.

After the work-ups had been completed, the boat would sometimes sit off Skye and the Kyle of Lochalsh, where on a couple of occasions during the summer months we had 'hands to bathe' (naval slang for going for a swim). This meant clambering up onto the casing and the foreplanes, which were the perfect height for a diving board, and diving in for a swim in the cold waters. The scenery was breath-taking, and these swims made such a difference to the crew, the sea temperature being just about bearable in the months of July and August. My heart pounded for a few seconds as I lay there floating without motion, allowing my body to relax and rally against the coldness. The Med it certainly wasn't, but as I pootled around looking at the haggardly beautiful landscape, the gin-clear water glistening in the sun, it was a rewarding end to what had been a week of hell. Seals could be seen in the distance, heads bobbing up and down as they no doubt wondered who these idiots were thrashing around.

The water I was swimming in contained the deepest reaches of UK territorial waters. The Inner Sound drops down to a tad over 1,050 feet in places and was used as a test-firing range for submarine torpedoes. I didn't think of that, though, as I slipped into a steady freestyle rhythm, moving away from the boat so I could just make out the sight of Skye's Old Man of Storr, an ancient landmark for mariners of a bygone age, gazing down on me, the water still as a millpond, the benevolent sun beating down. It didn't come much better than this, alone at last with nature, peace and quiet for half an hour. But I couldn't keep my eyes off the sleek, black bomber magnificently backdropped by Skye, the island's hills seemingly protecting her from the world beyond, this most secret weapon of war appearing shielded from prying eyes, except for a group of hikers on the shoreline who stood transfixed as they watched us out in the Sound.

Swimming back to the boat didn't have quite the same feeling about it, what with the dread of climbing back on board and descending into that smelly, cramped atmosphere, but at least I could dry off and spend some more time on the casing breathing in that wondrous fresh Scottish air. Just before I reached the sub I noticed that the TASO was fishing off the port side foreplanes and looked like he'd had some success; pollock, skate and mackerel were on the evening's menu.

A rope ladder was attached to the side of the boat so you could clamber back on board and dry off. After dinner it would be a riverboat ride to Portree, where we'd have a few jars in one of the pubs overlooking the harbour front. We could forget about the world for a few hours and the impending patrol. As I sat in the pub looking out to sea, the last remnants of evening sunlight struck the boat far out in the Sound, the gleaming leviathan strangely hypnotic against the fiery screen of a fading sky. It was soon time to get back on board for kick-off at 'zero six zero crack sparrow fart', as our very eccentric but brilliant XO referred to it. Then back to Faslane for the last pre-patrol repairs and missile load-up, before heading off into the abyss.

6

COULPORT

RNAD* Coulport filled me with both horror and joy. It was where the full magnitude of the job hit home as it was here that the boat was loaded with its nuclear arsenal. It wasn't all bad, though, as this was also the place we sailed back to after being on patrol to unload these messengers of death. Back in the 1980s it was one of the most secret military installations in the whole of Britain. Around eight miles from Faslane on the eastern side of Loch Long, Coulport was basically a long jetty. The Polaris missiles and their devastating warheads were kept in storage facilities very nearby. Before heading out on patrol we'd tie up alongside for two or three days as the missiles were loaded onto the boat through the hatches in the casing and into the missile tubes.

Apart from a very small number of people, no one knew just how many missiles were actually loaded onto the boat with warheads at the ready. This was because the missiles were shrouded by a protective covering, so you couldn't

* Royal Navy Armaments Depot.

actually pick out the Re-entry bodies which housed the warheads. I used to spend my watches as quartermaster trying to see if anything was actually going into the missile tube. I used to wonder, *Is it all a big bluff and we're not actually carrying any missiles at all?* But that was a vain hope. We always went on patrol with nuclear weapons. The missiles were brought down to the jetty on massive lorries from their hidden-away bunkers that had been built into the hills of the base, then transferred over by crane under the guidance of the WEO and his team. This was always quite a nerve-wracking procedure as the crane operator hoisted the deadly missiles from the jetty over to the casing. I'd look on in horror, trusting that the crane wouldn't buckle under the weight and drop one into the water. Now, that would have been a story.

Coulport was grim, no doubt about it. Bleak, brutal and usually overcast, the sky would have a dark, foreboding quality about it, a miserable steel grey, like the inside of an old saucepan, as if it had foreknowledge of what the next two or three months underwater had in store for me. I used to spend hours as quartermaster looking through my binoculars towards White Bay, Finart Bay and into Ardentinny Forest on the other side of Loch Long, convinced that Soviet spies were monitoring our every movement as we prepared the missiles. I mean, come on, they must have been. I'm sure they would have had reconnaissance patrols in that part of Scotland ever since the Polaris programme had begun. I thought the same when we left for patrol. After all, there were many farmhouses along the banks of Gare Loch, but who lived in them? And what about all the small boats we passed? Who was crewing them? We had no idea, and you could only assume that the Soviets were.

But it was the nights that really got to me. As QM, I'd stand on the jetty staring at the black bomber before me, her missile payload full, hoping to God that the next few months would pass without drama, that she'd look after us all and keep us safe and away from danger. That's all I ever wanted: no fuss, no surprises. Nowadays – well, at least before Putin's rise to power – it's hard to believe that nuclear war is remotely conceivable; but for this nervous, somewhat eccentric 19-year-old back then, it looked a very real possibility. One misconstrued order, Reagan trigger-happy in the White House with Thatcher at his every beck and call, the Soviets on the brink, rumours emerging weekly of the Russian military waiting in the wings, keeping an eye on Gorbachev and his reforms. Would he go too far for their liking? What would that lead to? Then we'd have all the hawkish headbangers in charge, ready to play their ultimate hand. Maybe they'd consider a first-strike option to wipe out the enemy. I'm sure I used to overthink all the different scenarios, but that was how I felt before most patrols. Broadcasting the fact that I thought both the president of the United States and our own prime minister to be major loons was probably not good for one's career prospects, so I kept these opinions very much to myself.

Before we went on patrol, we would occasionally receive a VIP visitor in a 'morale-boosting' exercise to see us gently off into that good night. They were usually mind-numbingly boring, generally some Rear Admiral or other. God forbid if he wasn't a submariner; his welcome would be openly hostile, the big 'fuck off' pill. They'd come on board and drone on and on about what a great job we were doing for both the Navy and the country, and it was neither morale-boosting nor the slightest bit interesting. They spent little time with the junior rates, and when they did it was always so stilted and staged and with more than a hint of condescension about it as we all stood around praying for it to end.

Two visits, however, live long in the memory. The first was a very senior cabinet minister of the day, who, although extremely charismatic and charming, had a low tolerance to alcohol, and over the course of an afternoon he proceeded to drink himself into a complete stupor with the senior and junior rates.

The visit had started well. He'd been taken on a brief tour of the boat, then he'd given a stirring speech about the self-sacrifice of submariners, what we have to go through to do the job we do, and how he, along with the support staff, our families and the nation held us in the highest of esteem knowing the harrowing responsibilities that rested on our shoulders. It was Churchillian stuff all right, far more inspiring than listening to some Admiral Toffington-Smythe waffle on; indeed, a couple of the crew to my left started to well up as his speech reached its climax, and there was wild cheering at its end. I didn't agree with everything he said – some bits were a tad jingoistic for my liking – but I had to admire the sheer coolness of the guy and how he immediately transfixed the crew. Tour concluded, speech over and on to the main business of the day – the drinking. It became clear after an hour or so that he was game for a session, and lunch was hastily put together for him in the senior rates' lounge to see if we could quell the effects of the booze. To no avail, though, for he/we ploughed on and by mid-afternoon he was paralytic and totally incoherent. It was then decided to get him onshore sharpish, before anything leaked out.

He couldn't get off the boat under his own steam, so I had the unenviable task of being underneath his left buttock, my shoulder heaving his scrawny arse out through the main access hatch, while he caterwauled about the need for just one more drink, demanding to see the skipper and raving wildly about Mrs Thatcher.

He was then carried over the gangway, a sailor under each arm, to an awaiting Navy bus and whisked away, never to be mentioned again. The only sight funnier than this was the following 30 minutes, as a wild-eyed coxswain bellowed his way through the submarine with murderous intent, looking for the chief culprits. Not very constructive, given he'd been sitting next to the VIP for most of the lunch, and had matched him drink for drink.

The second pre-patrol visit I remember was the PM herself, at Faslane. She was very petite but all hustle and bustle as she charged around the submarine, clambering up and down ladders, through bulkhead doors and in and out of the various compartments. I think it was her second visit to the boat, and by the looks of it she remembered where everything was.

I happened to be on the casing making my way off the boat to begin my quartermaster watch, when I started chatting to one of the WEMs (weapons engineering mechanics), who was checking the forward escape hatch. He needed to pass some equipment down the hatch to another mechanic below to wind up proceedings, and, well known for his short fuse, he was getting agitated wondering where his mate had gone. I looked down into the boat with him, and we both noticed a figure standing slightly under the hatch but further into the torpedo space, so we couldn't recognise them.

That was when he went mental: 'Whoever that is down there, get the fuck out of the way. You're blocking the hatch, you big cock splash!'

We both stood dumbstruck as Thatcher's aquiline face loomed into full view beneath us. 'Is everything all right, gentlemen?' she asked, peering upwards.

By this time we'd both vanished into thin air, fast. The WEM ran on board to hide, while I lay down and made myself small in the QM's cabin. Meanwhile, the coxswain was on the warpath looking for the two hooligans who had just abused the prime minister. Some moments later he pitched his head out of the main access, incoherently shouting at me as to whether I'd seen or heard anything. Pretending not to hear him, I waved back and smiled, thumbs up. He glared at me but had no proof of anything, so he disappeared back on board to continue the hunt.

7

BEFORE THE OFF

The last night before patrol was spent either on watch on board the submarine (unlucky) or ashore in Helensburgh (lucky) in the Imps – the Imperial Hotel – getting fully inebriated one last time before coming back on board by midnight and waking up with a hangover and a fried breakfast before setting sail. I experienced both over the years, and the evening out could either go very smoothly or it could be a night to remember for all the wrong reasons. Travelling back in a taxi on one occasion, very much the worse for wear, things were not quite right with one of the passengers, who was getting more and more annoyed with the driver. This passenger, a leading radio operator, hailed from the blue – Rangers – half of Glasgow, and he'd noticed some mini green-and-white-hooped boxing gloves hanging from the taxi driver's rear-view mirror, showing his support for rivals Celtic. He didn't wear that well, so he decided to set the driver's head on fire with a Zippo lighter from the backseat. Luckily, he was overpowered by the rest of us. I shudder to think what he would have done to me if I'd mentioned to him the Irish Catholic side of my family. Some things are best left unsaid.

On another drunken evening I was apprehended by two burly policemen for the classic sailor misdemeanour of pissing in a public place (well, not really, it was 30 yards down a back alley. I did at least try my best). The coxswain, who was out with me, told the police they had to let me go as I was driving the boat and was the only person who could manoeuvre her through the Rhu Narrows. All complete nonsense, of course, but it did the trick. Plod let me go and I avoided time in a prison cell the night before departure. The coxswain was surprisingly gracious about it and saw fit not to tell the captain, so I got away with it completely.

As QM, dealing with full-on, pissed-up sailors returning to the boat could be hard work – making sure they didn't fall overboard, start any fights, abuse the MOD police (easier said than done) or indeed give me any grief while getting back on board. Lots of us single guys used to volunteer to keep watch on the last night before a patrol to let husbands see their wives for a final time before they headed off to sea. It seemed like the right thing to do. To be brutally honest, given that service life involved being separated from loved ones for a very long time, I found it remarkable that any marriage could survive. The Submarine Service had the highest rate of divorce throughout the whole of the armed forces, but even so, many stood the test of time. It certainly took a remarkable type of woman to put up with a submariner as a husband.

As well as spending as much time as possible getting hammered, the last few days were dedicated to storing last-minute provisions, with engineers working overtime back aft to ensure that the reactor was fully operational and 'critical' – a confusing term in modern-speak, meaning it was creating enough nuclear fission to generate the power to propel the boat and run the life-support and other systems. This was crucial for obvious reasons; if the reactor was not running properly at sea, the submarine would have no power and be unable to function without using the diesel back-up, which would have been virtually impossible at periscope depth. Recharging the diesels was noisy and involved plumes of smoke coming out of the mast; not great if you're meant to be undetected on deterrent patrol. It had been done before, however. On *Resolution*'s first patrol she'd had problems with her CO_2 scrubbers not working correctly, so had spent a lot of time snorting at periscope depth to reboot the atmosphere throughout the boat. It could have endangered the very secrecy of the deterrent before it had even begun, but luckily for all, the boat remained undetected for the duration of the patrol.

8

SET SAIL

When the day finally came it was always one of mixed emotions. Leaving family and friends behind was tough, but to me it was far more that that; it was the thought of being shut off from the rest of world, disappearing for ten weeks or more at a time, with no contact, the only communication coming from the Command Centre at Northwood. The isolation was the killer; that, and dealing with over 140 sweaty blokes in a confined space in a fairly hostile living environment and finding ways to endure the lengthy periods of boredom that would no doubt feature heavily in the coming weeks, without becoming obsessed with the passing of time and constant clock-watching.

Before we set sail, the captain had his heads of department report to him that they were ready to go. The XO confirmed to the captain that the sub was ready for the off, after which we'd be all set to go to sea. The captain then made his way to the bridge where he was informed about the state of the propulsion system, the reactor and main engines by the navigating officer. The captain then assumed control of the boat and moved us out into Gare Loch with the help of tugs – submarines not being the easiest of vessels to move in and out from a jetty with a limited turning space. Finally, we were ready to commence what could be the ultimate defence of the realm.

We first moved quietly through the Rhu Narrows. On most patrols that I went on, family members of the crew would stand on Rhu Spit, a hinterland on the port side of the boat, and wave as *Resolution* slid effortlessly down the Narrows into the North Channel, always at a high tide so we didn't have the potential embarrassment of the capital ship running aground. It was the same every patrol – with very little fuss and no fanfare, this fierce black messenger of death slipped away. Families watching their loved one's departure from the shore were only told a couple of days

Resolution shows off for the cameras somewhere off
the west coast of Scotland.

before when the boat was actually leaving, as of course this was classified information.

There were several different routes to the open sea to keep the enemy – almost certainly monitoring our progress – on their toes. The boat pressed on, making its way to the North Channel, past Great Cumbrae, past the Isle of Arran and, leaving the Mull of Kintyre (forever in my memory from early childhood after the song by Paul McCartney) and Machrihanish behind us, we'd head past Rathlin Island into the North Atlantic, where we'd dive. We'd try to avoid the Soviet spy ship moored off the coast of Ireland at its most northerly point at Malin Head. It affected the pretence of being a fishing boat, but had so many aerials and other bits of communication equipment hanging off it, it couldn't have been anything other than an intelligence gatherer. It used to attempt to monitor the comings and goings of the bomber boats from Faslane, then relay that information back to the Soviet hunter-killers that must have been lurking off the coast to track our boat. The way to combat this was either with diesel-electric O-boats hassling the spy ship by taking photos through their peri-scopes in close proximity, or with our own hunter-killer subs noisily leading us out on patrol, allowing us to simply sneak out undetected.

Until we dived, the submarine would be very much like a surface ship. I had two main jobs when the boat was still above water: first, assisting with navigation in the control room on the plot, where bearing fixes such as landmarks, lighthouses and so on were taken on the periscope and matched with our on-board navigational aids to work out exactly where we were, then reported to the officer of the watch (OOW), who would be up in the conning tower in command of the boat. The conning tower – we used to call it 'the tube' – connected the control room and bridge, and is the shark-fin part of the submarine that sticks out of the water. Trying to keep on top of the navigation plot when the sea was in the grip of a ferocious swell could be an enlightening experience.

I'd never experienced seasickness before joining the Navy. The closest thing I'd suffered was as a little lad at the fairground, when my grandfather managed to get a Waltzer ride stopped after I became more and more uncomfortable with every revolution and started screaming with fear. When on the surface in rough waters, the boat soon turned into a disaster area. It used to roll and pitch, and on one particularly hideous journey out to a patrol we were moving around 20° to 30° on either side, a particularly nauseating motion. Mix this with the hot atmosphere below deck and the limited air coming through the conning tower, and you'd have at least three-quarters of the crew vomiting everywhere. It was hideous, like the worst hangover imaginable, but a hangover you'd had zero fun in earning. Entire areas of the boat were soon awash with spew, buckets strewn around everywhere and an intolerable stink rising, and anything that hadn't been correctly stowed was flying around, with men strapping themselves in to their bunks to try to avoid getting thrown out of their beds in the senior and junior rates' sleeping quarters.

My overall feeling of nausea, coupled with an increase in my saliva build-up, left me looking like a living corpse, gaunt and haggard, and it was all I could do to keep watch without surrendering to retching. While all of this was going on there was still a chef on watch in the galley at all times, cooking three meals a day for the 140-odd crew, although – like most others – I couldn't eat anything in heavy seas as I'd never have kept it down. These unsung culinary heroes were remarkable, cooking up fillet steak while trying to remain on their feet as pots and pans, cutlery and other utensils flew around them.

The other job I had while we headed out to our diving area was that of lookout on the bridge, which sat atop the conning tower, with the officer of the watch. This was a particular highlight, as I got on well with most of the crew in the bridge, particularly the navigating officer, a calm, sensible individual whom I liked a lot. We'd natter on to one another while taking in the majestic views of the west coast of Scotland. Arran, the largest island in the Firth of Clyde, is breathtaking, and there's surely no better place on earth to take your final look through binoculars before descending to the ocean depths. We'd be strapped in up there, as a lookout on HMS *Courageous* had once been lost to a massive 'goffer' – a large breaking wave – that literally sucked him out of the conning tower, never to be seen again.

On the odd occasion I'd see dolphins swimming along-side the boat; they'd ride the bow wave majestically and at great speed, effortlessly leaping out of the water, almost as if they were using the sub's bow wave as some decent surf. Feeling safe alongside their new friend, they'd do this for half an hour or so, then they'd be off as quickly as they appeared to another part of the vast ocean.

Keeping watch at night with the ship still surfaced was unbelievable. Looking out into the vast expanse of sky, I'd scan the constellations, trying to pinpoint various stars, searching for the Orion nebula and clusters like the Beehive. It was all the more unnerving, however, when I sat in complete darkness, the blackness above shot with shimmer-ing white dots, serenely beautiful like moondust. It was a feeling like nothing else on earth.

The submarine emitted barely any light apart from the port, starboard and aft safety lights on display. It was invis-ible to the world outside. And the only two noises you could hear were the Atlantic winds, ever increasing the further out to sea we sailed, coupled with the sound of the boat powering through the ocean, her bow hugging the water. I should have been keeping a look-out for potential threats of collision, but instead I was looking to the skies with wonder. I nearly came unstuck on one patrol when the OOW and I failed to see a submarine come down our starboard side about 400 yards away in the fading darkness. We spotted the display lights but didn't notice it was a sub until both vessels passed each other like, well, ships in the night. We waved, they waved back, us on our way out, them coming home. Good night – and good luck.

The other main plus about spending time on the bridge was that it gave me valuable time away from most of the crew, time virtually to myself, before we descended into the darkness. It was a time for reflection and thinking, not about the weeks ahead, for if I overthought things, the prospect of what we were about to do would become overwhelming. This was rather an opportunity to get rid of negative thoughts, as what was needed was positivity – a big dose of it – in order to face down the potential monotony of patrol. It was also good to get my last dose of vitamin D and collect myself before we dived. Being strong was the key; dwelling on the possible depression I might experience cooped up down there was no use to anyone. After two or three weeks underwater things can start to become a tad grim, and if you don't keep your mind occupied you can easily crack up.

9

THE DIVE

After a couple of days on the surface, the point of no return came, to the accompanying holler of 'Diving stations, diving stations' being piped throughout the boat. You then knew that it was time to get accustomed to the new world awaiting below. The captain would tell the OOW and lookouts to come down, and the lookouts would stand at the bottom of the conning tower, relaying the cries of the OOW to the captain as he shut, clipped and pinned the upper and lower lids of the tower. This was the final symbolic act before every patrol. Once the lower lid had been shut and pinned, the captain would spend a few moments at the periscope taking in reports that the boat was ready to dive, while I would be sitting in the control room either on the CEP* or on the fire-control panel, ready to start plotting any contacts once we were below the water.

The captain would then place the dive in the hands of the XO, with 'Number 1, dive the submarine' being the usual

---

* Contact evaluation plot.

instruction. To dive a submarine, the main requirement is to achieve negative buoyancy so the boat is heavier than the water outside and thus sinks. This is done by opening the main vents and filling the ballast tanks with water, which allows the boat to be controlled when diving.

When a submarine is on the surface, its ballast tanks are filled with air to create buoyancy so that the submarine's density is less than the water surrounding it and it floats. When under the waves, the trim tanks are used to maintain the correct balance of water to create neutral buoyancy so the boat has the same density as the sea outside and thereby achieves its cruising depth, one that could easily be sustained for a complete circumnavigation of the world's oceans. A quantity of compressed air is always kept in reserve for use in the event of an emergency surface procedure. Managing the trim requires years of experience to get right – and obviously the faster you go, the harder it is. Keeping a boat evenly trimmed underwater at speed is akin to trying to control an aircraft in the sky, with the rudder, foreplanes and the afterplanes looking after the direction and depth of the boat.

Although it's not that noticeable, there's a slight incline forward and a trace of movement when you're diving, a bit like descending in a very slow-moving lift. I remember on my first patrol being ever so slightly underwhelmed by the whole experience, the crew exuding a sense of professional nonchalance, everything slow and laborious. I was expecting more of a *Das Boot*-style dive at speed, with everyone hurtling to the front of the boat to weigh it down. I mentioned this to the coxswain at the time, telling him I thought it was a tad unsatisfying, to which he responded with a cool stare and said, 'Humph, you're a cunt.' Wise words indeed.

We would descend to around 100 feet and then immediately head back up to periscope depth, just to check the planes and integrity of the ship-control workings. Meanwhile, the captain sought assurances from the rest of the boat that there were no leaks, and while whirling around on the periscope he'd perform continuous sweeps of the horizon, checking for contacts. This wasn't the time for anything to go wrong. No fucks-up, not here, not now.

When the skipper was comfortable with the nature of the reports coming back to him, it was time to go. The periscope was lowered, and then it was goodbye world. Everyone knew the submarine was now going to take on a bow-down angle and had to ensure everything was stowed away – this should have already been sorted on work-up, but you never can tell what might suddenly come loose – particularly something weighty that might prang someone on the head; one time a junior mechanic got struck by a flying monkey wrench on dive that had been left on top of the ship's systems console, receiving a sore head and a cut ear for his trouble.

There was a small symbol of the boat on the console in various degrees of pitch that had to be monitored. There would be another round of post-diving checks throughout each department, which would each then report back to the XO confirming there were no leaks. Sooner or later the boat would reach our operational patrol diving depth, which remains secret as it could jeopardise present or future submarine operations.

The workings of the ballast and trim tanks took place in the control room at the systems console, opposite to where I kept my watch. Forward of the missile compartment, this was the engineering heart of the boat. And while the reactor and all the associated systems were controlled back aft in the manoeuvring room, the systems console was good old-fashioned submarine engineering and controlled by the PO or chief stoker, along with a junior-rate stoker who'd help him out. I got a migraine just looking at all the controls and switches. One wrongly pulled switch, and chaos could ensue.

When we first dived on patrol, the submarine was at its maximum weight, burdened with three months' food and supplies. Gradually, food supplies got eaten, the sewage tank filled with waste and needed to be evacuated, so seawater was taken in to create fresh water and help in the production of oxygen. This all had to be considered when attempting to keep the submarine neutrally buoyant. Water was pumped by the use of the trim pump from forward to aft, or vice versa, to compensate for any increase or decrease in weight. This was done pretty constantly throughout the patrol, with small adjustments of water distribution here and there to make sure the submarine kept to an even keel.

The hover pump – yes, the submarine could hover – was controlled from the systems console as well and was used in the missile-firing procedure since the boat had to be stationary while firing, and it did this by the activation of the hover pump. The hydraulics system was located here too. Hydraulics is basically high-pressure oil that flows through various pipes from a central pumping plant to help operate certain equipment on board such as the steering gear, the planes, periscopes and masts, together with various flood and vent valves. The advantage of hydraulics is that its noise signature is very low, maintenance is straightforward for skilled engineers and the system does not get degraded by contact with seawater.

The systems console was the bread and butter of the forward engineering on the boat, and the marine engineers who looked after it took everything in their stride, were never stressed, always of a cheerful disposition and never ones for moaning, despite the difficult, hot and cramped working conditions. They'd be diving the boat one minute, sorting out the hydraulics the next, operating the laundry and clearing the toilets if they were backed up with shit, not to mention maintaining the battery if we needed back-up diesel power. All in a day's work without complaint, 24/7, week in, week out.

Watching the dolphins and constellations already seemed a long time ago. We were in the depths now, with 80 days ahead of us, hidden and cut off from the world – but for the communication from the Command Centre at Northwood.

Even though the public back home were unaware of the fact, this Cold War was actually very hot for the Polaris crews. Since 1968 when the patrols started, the officers and men of all the deterrent patrols – across Polaris and then Trident – have been on a constant war footing. Our response would have been quick and indeed brutal if the signal ever came, although I never really thought about it a great deal at the time, bizarre as that seems.

I could deal with the long absences, not being one to miss family and friends too much. It might sound harsh and uncaring, and I hadn't really recognised this part of me before I went out on patrol, but I was never overcome with feelings of homesickness – I suppose I must have been a bit of a loner. Maybe it was because I realised that if I was to survive weeks on end under the sea, all those people who were closest to me were best forgotten about.

10

A BRIEF TOUR

Once we'd dived, it was time to settle into the environment that would become home for the next three months. This seems like the best time for me to explain the main compartments within the submarine and give you a very brief description of what went on in each. Basically, the boat was split into three separate parts: front section – living, fighting, sleeping, washing, working, engineering, eating and entertaining; middle section – Armageddon (the missiles); back section – reactor, life-support services and propulsion. Let's start with everything forward of the missile compartment. This was the fighting hub of the submarine – its controls, the tactical heart of the boat, home of the attack team, and also where we ate, slept, shat, washed and entertained.

The nerve and command centre of the boat was ship control, situated in the Control Room and operated by a two-man band. It was from here that the submarine was manoeuvred and changed depth, as well as made changes to its course, all of which were dictated by the duty OOW, XO or captain. The foreplanesman was responsible for depth changes by manoeuvring the foreplanes up or down, and for changes in course to port and starboard by operation of the rudder. The afterplanesman was responsible for keeping the boat level at differing depths, most notably periscope depth, and for maintaining the degree of pitch within the correct parameters so the boat remained stable, particularly when diving or returning to periscope depth. It was essential he kept the correct angle on the boat, and the two men needed to work in perfect harmony to ensure the boat was at the right depth and angle, and on course. Failure to do this, especially at periscope depth, made them an easy target for the wrath of the skipper or XO if the periscope dipped in and out of the water, or conversely, we were too deep, so the captain couldn't see anything at all.

Ship control in many ways resembled an aircraft cockpit, with the foreplanesman sitting in the right-hand seat and the afterplanesman in the left-hand seat. Both used joysticks reminiscent of a commercial airliner as they soared through the ocean depths.

When the boat dived in normal patrol conditions, a form of autopilot was available that engaged both a fixed depth and a pre-set angle, so that the operation could be performed by a single person. Behind the autopilot, on the port-facing forward side, was the systems console, which was operated by the chief or petty officer stoker, with another stoker doing checks. It was usually manned by two sailors when on patrol, three if we were doing a run to periscope depth. I've touched on the systems console already; black in appearance, with switches everywhere, it looked like the sort of panel you'd find in an East European electric power plant in the 1960s. Buttons and switches had to be selected at the right time, in the right sequence, otherwise you could have a mini shit-storm on your hands, most notably when blowing the slop, drain and sewage tank to expel everyone's waste. As well as all the diving and surfacing shenanigans, it was from here that the periscopes – both attack and search – were raised and lowered.

When on patrol the submarine used SINS (ship's inertial navigation system), which through motion and rotation, computerised sensors and dead reckoning was able to continuously calculate the position of the submarine regardless of any movement. SINS was a mixture of accelerometers and gyroscopes mounted on a stable platform, which provided latitude and longitude, heading, speed and depth, and this would all feed into the navigation room and the missiles to give an accurate picture of where we were. If *Resolution* circumnavigated the world without ever once returning to periscope depth, SINS would need to be accurate to around 200 to 300 yards, to permit a sufficiently precise missile launch. A back-up to this was a regular return to periscope depth, where we would raise the BRN mast* and take a location pinpoint from global positioning

---

* At periscope depth, the BRN mast supplies the submarine with instantaneous navigation information to lock down its latitude and longitude.

satellites that locked down our position to within a few feet, after which it would be time to run off deep and hide sharp-ish. The computers that fed the missile systems would be constantly updated, as it was essential that the missiles knew the exact navigational position of the submarine prior to launch, so they could home in precisely on the target and not end up redecorating a vast expanse of the Soviet tundra.

The nav centre was a highly restricted space that was out of bounds to unauthorised personnel as it contained infor-mation on our patrol location. Where the submarine went on patrol was a secret closely guarded from most of the crew; only around a dozen men had access to the nav centre, and apart from the captain, XO and navigator, none of them knew our exact location. To preserve the secrecy of the boat's position, the charts in this room were always displayed upside down to deter anyone from taking a peek.

The middle of the control room was where you'd find that iconic piece of submarine kit everyone is familiar with, the attack and search periscopes. Periscopes in submarines date back to 1888 – the French experimental submarine *Gymnote* had one fitted – but it wasn't until the First World War that periscopes started to have a serious impact militarily, as submarines from both sides quickly gained a reputation for stealth and cunning. They have been a mainstay of operations ever since, and are used for navigation, safety and warfare (ranging and targeting). The attack periscope on *Resolution* was seldom used, mostly on exercise in work-up or if we were taking part in war games – I remember helping with an attack that 'sank' an aircraft carrier off the west coast of Scotland on one particular frantic afternoon's exercise.

Our very eccentric but legendary XO of the time said: 'Stand by to surface and machine gun survivors.' I think at least half of the crew thought he meant it. The attack periscope was longer and thinner than the search periscope, so the submarine could attack any potential targets from greater depth, and it was a lot smaller at the top, so was much harder to spot by any ships or planes that might have been out looking for us. It was monocular and fitted with various navigational aids, including a split-image rangefinder and horizon sextant, and had a de-icer for the top window, if required in colder climes.

The search periscope was binocular and bigger than the attack periscope, thus increasing the boat's vulnerability when used at periscope depth as it was more conspicuous. If we weren't at precisely the right depth near the surface, it could stick out above the water like a bulldog's balls. It was, however, the normal choice for the captain whenever we returned to periscope depth; since it had a larger diameter than the attack periscope but retained the same level of magnification, it made for good, sound visuals, making it much more comfortable to use.

To the right of the periscopes, on the starboard side of the control room, was the CEP (contact evaluation plot), where I spent the majority of my time on the submarine when on watch. Here contacts were plotted in real-time in relation to the position of the submarine. Behind and to the right of this was the computerised fire-control system (which I also worked on), whose sole purpose was using different algorithms to work out the course, speed and range of any new contact picked up by the sound room to aid the captain in getting an overall tactical picture.

Next to the fire-control system heading aft was the underwater telephone. It tended to be left on for all of the patrol, which meant I could hear all the multifarious sounds of the deep. Behind that was the ARL (Admiralty Research Laboratory) table that was used on the surface for plotting the bearings for fixes taken from the periscope; it doubled as the LOP* when we dived, which was another time-bearing plot. Though seldom used, with the advent of the fire-control system it was another way of helping the captain work out a potential target's course, speed and range, and was particularly useful when dealing with fast-moving vessels.

Finally, mounted against the wall in the control room, behind the LOP, was the bathythermograph. This was used to measure a combination of the water temperature and the velocity of sound in water while the boat traversed different depths of the oceans. A change of temperature in the sea from the surface to the different depths of a submarine's operating spectrum causes thermoclines, the transient layers between warmer and colder water temperature that

* Local operations plot.

make it possible for a submarine to hide away, as they can impair sonar performance for the hunter. Sonar works effectively if the sub has a highly reflective steel surface and is in water of the same temperature as that from which the initial sonar waves are transmitted; in this case the sound waves will bounce off the target and go straight back to the ship.

Some oceans vary in temperature and, consequently, so does the speed at which sound travels through their water. Conditions where there is little temperature change from surface to operating depth are known as 'isothermal', which is bad news for a submarine being hunted as the sonar is clear. Ideally, what a submarine needs is a layer of the ocean with a rapid increase or decrease in water temperature over a few feet. Diving below this layer can significantly reduce the chances of being detected … so the deeper the better.

We took readings by inserting a card into the bathythermograph every time we went to periscope depth, checking whether any new thermoclines had developed. Also, as the nuclear deterrent, we had access to historical data collected by submarines over the years to use in our search for depth perfection and the best methods of avoidance.

Moving out of the control room towards the front of the boat on the same deck, we come to the electronic countermeasure office, which was manned at periscope depth by the tactical systems team, in which I served. This was used in conjunction with the electronic warfare mast, which would be raised by the captain to check whether there were any ships or planes in the area operating radar; we'd be able to pick up the strength of any signal or determine how close the contact might be.

Moving further forward, there was a locked room where the navigator kept his various charts to help us with plotting our way to and from the patrol area on the surface. Through the passage directly underneath the main access hatch, the wireless room and sound room stood opposite to one another. The sound room was quite simply the eyes – and indeed ears – of the submarine. When a sub is submerged, its main gatherer of information in relation to sound outside the pressure hull is sonar. Sounds are picked up using hydrophones mounted near or around the bow that are then translated into visual data by computers in the sound room and interpreted by the sonar chief/petty officer of the watch and his team. This in turn would be passed on to the control room, where the tactical systems team would do its best to track the target and work out its own range, course and speed.

Passive sonar worked best under a speed of 5 to 6 knots, and we usually operated below that speed at no more than walking pace to gain the maximum benefit. Active sonar emits a 'ping' (like you hear in *Das Boot* or the old John Mills war films) when sonar waves bounce off any target, making its range much easier to calculate, but in turn it can quickly give the boat's position away due to the beam of energy – the ping – getting picked up by another submarine or boat. Listening passively means you're relying on any contacts making enough noise, either generated by the sound of machinery or the propeller, to then filter through to your sonar, which can be operated at any depth.

Operators also looked out for what is known as the 'Doppler effect', which in simple terms is the increase in frequency of sound as something comes towards the boat, and the decrease as it moves away. This is part of the 'Doppler shift', when a contact being tracked either at periscope depth or in the deep suddenly alters course; the skipper would then have a shit fit because he'd have to use his self-taught computational skills (albeit honed to perfection) to work out new fire-control solutions on the target, with the aid of his attack team.

The wireless room, slightly aft of the sound room, was strictly out of bounds to non-authorised personnel. Manned by the radio operators, it was here that all the signals and general patrol information came in from Northwood, including 'familygrams' we received from our next of kin every seven to ten days or so. The captain would also receive general information from here about ship or submarine movements, whether hostile or friendly, that could encroach on our patrol area. All the signals that were transmitted from Command Centre at Northwood would be sent at low frequency and be picked up by the comms wire we trailed out the back of the submarine just below the surface of the water, then relayed to the eager beavers in the wireless room. While essential in terms of maintaining contact with Northwood, the comms wire rendered the submarine considerably longer, which made manoeuvring the boat particularly challenging.

Even without the comms wire deployed, when operating in the fishing waters of the Atlantic off the Irish coast, the potential risk of getting tagged in nets was pretty substantial. There have been a few occasions when subs have dragged along fishing vessels, having become entangled, even pulling them into the deep with tragic loss of life.

On one occasion a fishing vessel was visible through the periscope for a couple of days, constantly following us; every change of course we made, she followed suit, until it suddenly dawned on us, and indeed the fishing vessel, that we were dragging it around like a killer whale with its prey. We had it by the nets, and thank goodness their captain cut them away, otherwise we'd have provoked a national scandal: Nuclear Deterrent Drags Hard-Working Fishermen to Davy Jones's Locker. The MOD would of course have denied all knowledge, I'm sure; they hardly ever comment on submarine operations, and when they do they're fairly economical with the truth, working on a need-to-know basis with the premise that there's seldom any need. Joe Public rarely needs to know much.

The sonar console space was the furthest forward on 1 Deck. As well as the mass of electronics needed to make the sonar work, it also housed air-cooled sonar. It proved to be a good place to hang out if I wanted some private time or to revise, both on my first patrol when I was studying for my dolphins badge and when I took educational qualifications later on in my service.

Let's now head down to 2 Deck. From the missile compartment, work forward on the port side and you'll find the captain's cabin, the wardroom and the officers' sleeping quarters. The captain was the only crew member with his own cabin, and from here he was able to listen in on all communications in order to keep abreast of developments when he wasn't in the control room. There was a safe in his cabin where his instructions concerning where to go while on patrol were kept. Adjacent to the Captains cabin were the officers' sleeping quarters, washrooms and toilets, all in close proximity, which was a fairly sobering experience, smell-wise. Officers ate every night in the wardroom, their meals having been prepared in the galley. I always found it amusing that grown men had to be waited on hand and foot in order to eat, but it was just part of the 'toff and oik' culture that was so prevalent in the British military at the time. I guess I simply never understood it. I was as much a stickler for Navy tradition as the next man, and I'm sure they were good at their jobs, but did they really need silver service deep under the North Atlantic?

On the starboard side working forward, you had the sick bay, the ship's office and the coxswain's office. The sick bay was obviously the doctor's domain. I was never sure if someone became seriously ill what the precise position would have been; whether you'd have tried to get the casualty off the boat or just insisted on the doc carrying out an emergency operation. Appendicitis was the main worry, and I do know subsequent to my time on board that an XO I served with, who went on to command the Trident submarine HMS *Vengeance*, surfaced on patrol and had a sailor with appendicitis taken off the boat by helicopter. Wise choice. Of course, there was the other choice too – just don't get ill.

The coxswain's office was where the chief of the boat hung out. When I was doing my Part 3 training to qualify I'd go there once a week, full of dread and often despair, for him to test me on some hydraulic system, or in what sequence the ventilation fans would be restarted after an emergency, or about the rush escape procedure, or how torpedoes were fired. He always liked to end the meeting with a damage-control-type scenario, to which I'd be expected to know the answer.

'Right, Humph. Two a.m. collision with a submarine at 200 feet, water starts pissing into the control room … you've got ten seconds, what you gonna do? Ten, nine, eight …'

I'd sit there, clueless, thinking I'd either be dead or sucked out into the sea, all the while going redder and redder trying to think of a smart-alec reply or something more intelligent. It was soul-destroying.

Then he'd just say, 'You've fucked it, Humph, lost the whole crew. And it's all your fault.'

Death by humiliation. Not that he ever held a grudge; it would all be forgotten 20 minutes later as he started on some other unfortunate trainee hunting for his dolphins.*

The ship's office was used by the petty officer chef, who'd be working out how many more tins of steak and kidney pud he had left and exactly when the eggs were going to run out; or the supply officer would be in there worrying when the loo roll would start having to be rationed. The leading writer would also use the office, to keep the boat's administration ship-shape and up to date.

You then moved forward to the senior rates' mess. Fitted out with a bar, it also doubled up as an operating theatre if required. Opposite was the upper senior rates' bunk space and their annex, where the coxswain held court. At the bottom of the ladder from 1 Deck on the port side was the garbage ejector space, which quite literally used to fire out the rubbish – known as 'gash' – to the depths. Nowadays, to comply with international law, some of the gash is kept on board until the submarine returns to port. In my day it was broken down in a grinder and ejected via a vertical tube, the gash gun, having first been weighed down so it would sink all the way to the ocean floor. Also down here was the precipitator room, where high-voltage precipitators using electricity to attract dust particles removed them from the atmosphere.

Next, the galley directly in front was where a team of three chefs under the guidance of the petty officer chef

* There was usually around 5 to 10 per cent of the crew who were studying for their dolphins on any given patrol.

would work wonders creating culinary delights for the crew in a small kitchen approximately 15 square feet in size. The meals were rich, plentiful and varied – an amazing feat when concocted in such conditions.

Opposite the galley was the junior rates' mess, where I tucked in to all my meals. The mess also doubled up as the main entertainment area in the boat, with quizzes, horse-racing nights, soap operas and cinema nights, when the latest Hollywood films were shown on two-spool cinema reels. It felt a bit like going to a small old-fashioned village hall with a pull-down screen, except we were deep under the

The wonderful chefs undertaking food prep in the very confined space of the galley.

North Atlantic. We also had keep-fit classes in there, and a religious service on a Sunday for anyone who felt the need.

Back to the port side now, and just forward of the galley was the scullery – with the garbage grinder – and the ship's canteen, from which you could buy sweets and 'goffa' (fizzy drinks), booze and 'snadgens' (cigarettes). I'd run up a tab over the course of the patrol – easily a couple of hundred quid if the drink got the better of me – and I paid it off when I got back to shore. Between the scullery, galley and the pressure hull was the provisions store, which kept all the non-perishable food stuffs required for patrol.

Just before entering the torpedo compartment (the fore ends), the most forward part of the boat, there was a small hatch going down to 3 Deck that housed the freezer compartment and sufficient refrigerator space for the perishable foods, all mercilessly crammed in so we'd never grow hungry. It would also be used on rare occasions to temporarily house a dead body, should anyone be unfortunate enough to pop their clogs while at sea. I'm not too sure what the chefs would have made of it, though, clambering over a dead body to get to the frozen fish of the day. Fortunately, in my career we never had a patrol death.

Let's now pass into the torpedo compartment through a bulkhead door. The boat was sub-divided into areas with bulkheads, giving the submarine an added safety feature; if there was a flood it could be contained by shutting the bulkheads and isolating the compartment where it occurred, then blowing the ballast tanks and returning to the surface *tout suite*. An issue certainly could have arisen, however, if the flooding was rapid and heavy; then people situated in the non-escape compartments of the submarine would have had a good chance of drowning. Hopefully, the boat would be in shallow enough water that an escape could be attempted via the escape hatches by the crew left in either of its ends. If not, the boat would implode at crush depth, so being in the escape hatches would be pointless anyhow, as the boat would be traversing at great speed and a rush escape futile and impossible.

The torpedo compartment was itself split into two decks. The bottom one was the business end where torpedoes were fired from their tubes. These tubes were basically an extension of the pressure hull, and to prevent flooding they had an inner (breech) and outer door (muzzle), which were opened and closed at different times. A torpedo was launched by equalising the pressure inside the tube with that of the seawater outside. The muzzle door opened and a water ram system thrust the torpedo out of the tube and away it went, wire-guided to the target.

If we had any extra guests on board, or there were more Part 3 trainees than usual, they'd have to sleep on camp beds down here, where they'd enjoy absolutely no privacy whatsoever. You'd have to get some kip under the rowdy junior rates' space, nodding off to the loungy soundtrack of some 70s porn. In the rec space above, alongside the porn, movies were watched, and cards and 'uckers' – a board game very similar to Ludo – were played. It also doubled as the ship's library, and was where all interviews for promotions or gaining your dolphins badge took place. Its other main military function was as the home of the forward escape compartment, which entered around the main escape hatch. For support there were oxygen generators, CO_2 absorption units and oxygen-burning candles. The upper level was also full of air pipes and connections for breathing units, both static and portable, enabling the crew to breathe in the event of an escape.

Down to 3 Deck now, where from forward to aft it was another senior rates' bunk space, as well as the laundry. This ran a couple of times a week for shirts, T-shirts and trousers, usually on a Monday, then overalls from the engineers on a Tuesday, to get the stench out. Within a couple of hours of putting on clean shirts, the tell-tale BO and sweat would return. Moving aft, the junior rates' bunk spaces were spread over most of the remainder of the deck. You slept in close proximity to other members of your team so you were all together and easier to locate when woken up to go on watch. The bunks were small, with barely enough room to lie either on your side or flat on your back without your nose being squashed against the Formica of the bunk above. It was pitch-black down there, so sleeping was easy, although the dreams and the nightmares came easily too. The junior rates' toilets, showers and washroom were also along here, as was the main battery under 3 Deck, in the event that we had to switch to diesel power instead of nuclear.

Still on 3 Deck, right outside 9 Berth (my bunk space), was AMS 1 (auxiliary machinery space), which housed a hydraulic plant, together with bilge and ballast pumps. Further aft, indeed as aft as you could go, was the missile control centre, where the missile trigger was kept. It was here, in conjunction with the control room, that the countdown to launch was managed. In this event, the WEO would sit and launch the missiles by firing a trigger, which was normally kept in a safe.

Coming out of the missile centre was a ladder to the port side that went back on itself up to 2 Deck. Climbing it, you

Inside the missile control centre as a practice drill is being carried out. Seated nearest to the camera is the WEO with his hand on the firing trigger, ready to go.

couldn't help but stare – gobsmacked – into the missile compartment. Effectively the middle of the boat, it spanned three decks and was large enough to house 16 Polaris missiles, each 9.5m high, 1.4m in diameter and weighing 1,270kg. On the middle deck, those on watch kept vigil behind a roped-off area out of bounds to most of the crew. Here the temperatures of the missile tubes and the general compartment environment were monitored; the personnel also played a key role in the firing sequences of the missile tubes and the flooding of the tubes before launch. If a submariner breached this unauthorised area he'd be met with sudden and decisive truncheon blows and a subsequent thick ear, at best.

The health physics lab, also situated in the missile compartment, was where medical and radiological worlds collided, in the form of monitoring everyday life threats on board – testing oxygen, nitrogen, hydrogen and CO_2 levels throughout the boat to ensure they were within sufficiently safe limits to maintain life under the sea. The tech office, again situated in the missile compartment, housed thousands of different items to repair any defects that might occur on patrol (spare valves to operate the flushing mechanism for the toilets being one).

Exiting the missile compartment, heading aft, you came to AMS 2, the chief life-systems area of the boat, where the marine engineering mechanics maintained the ship's atmosphere-purification equipment. On 1 Deck you had three CO_2 scrubbers, whose job was to remove the dangerous CO_2 exhaled by the crew from the boat's atmosphere.

Sitting opposite the CO_2 scrubbers were two electrolysers, which supplied oxygen to the crew by the electrolysis of water particles, producing oxygen. Also on 1 Deck was a CO/H_2 burner, whose function was to remove carbon monoxide and hydrogen from the ship's atmosphere, while on 2 Deck the toxins created by refrigerants or aerosols were dealt with by the Freon removal plants. Aerosols were banned, so the only acceptable alternative was roll-on deodorants, not that these helped much in preventing the rank pong of human sweat. On 3 Deck sat the two diesel generators that would be used in the event of a reactor shutdown or loss of nuclear propulsion. Also in AMS 2 were the de-humidifiers, whose task was to remove moisture particles from the boat, keeping condensation off the machines and their electrical supply.

Coming back up to 1 Deck, looking aft, you were faced with the reactor compartment. The reactor – effectively a latter-day steam engine – supplied steam through the heat generated by nuclear fission, which in turn produced the power driving the propulsion turbines and electrical generators to make the boat function. The only way to get aft of the submarine was via the tunnel across the top of the reactor compartment. When I first went through it as a wide-eyed 18-year-old, I was unsure as to whether I was actually passing into the reactor itself, so I just stood there outside the bulkhead, gawping into the tunnel, waiting like the new boy at school for someone to come through from the other side and show me how to enter. You have to open one bulkhead door, walk through and close it behind you, before going through to open the other bulkhead door. This was to minimise any potential radiation or safety breaches. The crew were protected against adverse radiation by primary and secondary shielding around the reactor itself, and then around the steam generator and main coolant pump. The big plus about the reactor was that it gave the submarine the ability to operate independently of the earth's atmosphere for extended periods of time, as the generation of nuclear power needed neither oxygen nor air to make it work.

Once out of the tunnel you arrived in AMS 3, which was dominated by the manoeuvring room. In here, among all the dials that gave the impression of a mini power station, a team of engineers and artificers controlled all the nuclear, electrical and propulsion needs of the boat (the actual speed of the submarine was regulated here by the throttles). There were so many dials and controls it brought me out in a rash of hives when I first saw it; I thought I'd never remember them all for my qualification exams, but during my first patrol it grew to be the area I most enjoyed visiting. I found it fascinating to see how everything came together mechanically here, so far away from my job at the other end of the boat. I loved getting my overalls and boots on too, clambering about back aft and learning about nuclear propulsion, measuring pressures, flows, temperatures, precipitation, electrolysers and the like. It was all good, so long as I didn't touch anything.

On 2 Deck of AMS 3 were generators and auxiliary motors; also found here was various equipment for safeguarding the running of the nuclear reactor. On 3 Deck lived the two turbo generators, and when the reactor was critical – i.e. up and running – they supplied all the boat's electrical functions from the heat/power generated by the reactor.

Out of AMS 3 going further aft, you found yourself in the engine room, which housed the main turbines that drove the submarine. The final compartment in the arse-end of the boat was the motor room, where the electrical propulsion motor and clutch shaft were, doubling up as the aft escape compartment. It was also where the horribly cramped after escape hatch was situated. I used to have nightmares about being stuck back aft in a flood or fire and having to escape from the motor room – nigh on impossible as it was so claustrophobic; the mere thought of it was enough to affect the deepest of sleeps.

All the associated gear to turn the propeller was here, and considering that the propeller powered the boat along it was fairly quiet. I used to worry about the propeller's shaft, as it penetrated the pressure hull to connect it to the blades of the propeller itself and had an extra sealing on it to prevent leaks. Any weakness in said sealing, and seawater would immediately start pissing into the compartment, filling the boat in seconds. The seal did actually leak some water, which would accumulate in the bilges and then get pumped overboard. The same could be said for other major penetrations of the pressure hull, like the torpedo tubes or the periscopes, and it could be fairly unnerving keeping watch in the control room if we were running at ultra-quiet stage, and thus fairly deep, with water coming down the periscopes and into the well.

Sometimes sailors – including myself – would be lowered into the well to clean up the water so the periscope itself wouldn't be damaged. It was a tight fit, and I could barely move my hands in front of my body to wipe away the hydraulic oil. The periscope would be raised and the hydraulics isolated, and I would then have to clamber down on a flimsy rope ladder and commence the clean-up while hoping the periscope didn't drop down on my head.

This was my living environment for three months at a time. I remember once diving in May and next seeing daylight in August, just shy of 100 days, a seriously long time to be running around cut off from the world. Miles and miles of pipes, high-pressure air, fans, pumps, nuclear weapons, an on-board nuclear reactor, 143 men, all stuffed within a pressurised hull and then dunked into the corrosive water of the world's saltwater oceans. It's a wonder any of us ever ventured in there in the first place.

11

NO TIME

How much do you take for granted when you throw back the curtains on a beautiful sun-drenched morning and feel yourself at one with the world? Or when you step out at night into the garden and gaze up at the countless constellations of stars? Or even when you're aware that it's breakfast, lunch or dinner time; having a lovely long shower or bath; sitting in the park soaking up the sun; or simply knowing where you are now, and where you'll be in the future? All are fundamentals of human life, but when submerged deep underwater as a submariner, they seem like priceless luxuries you once enjoyed in some dim and distant past long ago.

I suppose the closest feeling approximating to being on a submarine as a civilian would be to imagine spending a quarter of a year on a tube train or airliner. And whether you will flourish or not is all down to a matter of temperament – being able to cope with long, often dull periods of time under the sea. No one could have prepared me for it. In fact, no amount of training at submarine school can prepare anyone for the torturous mental strain of being up to three months away at sea; certainly no one at HMS *Dolphin* taught me how to keep my shit together for weeks on end without going stir crazy, or how to keep life interesting despite the daily grind and the inevitable monotony of much of the work. That was down to me.

On board the submarine, once we'd dived on patrol, I had no sense of time whatsoever. It was akin to being buried at sea. There were – obviously – no portholes to see out of. Oddly, this used to be the question most often asked when people visited: 'Why aren't there any windows so you can see where you are?' We never deigned to answer. There was no resemblance to a normal day in this timeless, windowless existence under the ocean, made doubly worse by not knowing where the hell you were. Imagine being lost at sea, all hands perished and, since it was top secret, our final resting place never to be revealed to loved ones. When you put all these factors together with the regimented watch-keeping environment, trying to keep abreast of the time became quite challenging, if not impossible.

The 24-hour day centred around a watch pattern that played havoc with my body rhythms. The watch system followed one of two patterns, known as 'one in two' and 'one in three'. One in two was the killer – either six hours on, six off, or four hours on, four off. We usually did this on work-up while we got the sub, and ourselves, ready for patrol. After a few days of one in two and the fitful sleep you managed to get, you'd end up looking like a living corpse:

red eyes, bad breath, and constipation or shitting for England. It was like being in prison; you were either in bed or on watch. There'd be no time for any sort of social life after coming off watch – just grab some food, a quick drink and then head down. It took its toll, the sheer monotony of it, and I reckon I'd have completely cracked up if it had gone on for a full patrol. On patrol, we tended to do more one in threes, so I'd do four hours on, eight hours off. With one in three watches, we'd fix it that every third day you'd run a longer watch, so the watch finishing at 8 p.m. would get 12 hours off … party time! This was operationally invaluable, as it meant a whole 24-hour period could run on just three watches, vital in the cramped and confined space of a submarine with limited crew.

The constant grind of that never-ending schedule could be terribly disconcerting. I'd wake thinking it was time for breakfast, and then on arrival at the galley I'd be faced with steak and kidney pud followed by apple crumble and custard – the only meal on offer as it was 8 p.m. I had to eat it, though, otherwise I wouldn't get anything for another 12 hours, and food times were one of the only pleasant things to look forward to.

Coping with the watch system was the main obstacle to overcome on patrol. This wasn't a problem on my very first trip as I had to do a six-hour watch, come off, then get my overalls on and spend three to four hours back aft in the engineering spaces, learning about the basics of nuclear fission, propulsion, steam generators and the like, or I'd be in the missile compartment or forward somewhere learning about the missiles, hydraulics and other major hull valves and machinery. It was a fucking nightmare, constantly on the go, my head and arse buried in some dark, dank recess of AMS 3 trying to learn as much as I could about how the submarine operated, then grabbing any bits of sleep when I could. That said, in many respects managing time was a lot easier when I was inexperienced, although because the pressure was on to qualify and I had a massive workload, I was lucky if I got more than six hours' sleep in any given 24-hour period

I worked hard and had a good, positive attitude. What else can you do? No point moping around, and remember, I was the lowest of the low, just setting out, so it was important to create the right impression. Most of the crew were very helpful, as I studied for my dolphin badge to become a fully fledged submariner, but there was a small handful who were complete arseholes and thought it was amusing to take the mickey out of this young lad from the Black Country. They were mostly dinosaurs who'd been on bombers for, say, 10 to 15 years and thought every new Part 3 trainee was sub-human scum they wouldn't waste their breath on. But I didn't let it get under my skin. Piss-take, abuse, humiliation – it was a pretty sad state of affairs when someone's main aim on patrol was to make all the new guys feel worthless, and usually in front of fellow shipmates. I never could work that out, but I suppose in many ways they'd become institutionalised by the Navy and thought belittling and humiliating junior rates was an acceptable way to behave.

My education at boarding school helped me to survive. I'd been used to this sort of abuse so could take it in my stride. The arseholes were very much the minority, however, and most of my fellow crewmates were glad to assist in any way they could to help me qualify as a submariner.

Every Part 3 trainee had a mentor to see them through their first patrol and hopefully towards qualification. I was lucky to have Leading Seaman Philip Atkins in my corner. A Geordie stalwart of both diesel and hunter-killer submarines, he was new to Polaris submarines like I was, but that's where the similarities ended. He was already nearing legendary status among submariners, as he had been periscope assistant on HMS *Conqueror* at the time of the Falklands War and had been on the other side of the periscope from the captain on that fateful day in May 1982 when *Conqueror* sank the *General Belgrano*. It was then – and still is to this day – the only time a British submarine has sunk an enemy ship since the end of the Second World War. He had forearms like Popeye, and when he spoke everyone shut up; he was clearly highly thought of by both officers and ratings for what he'd been through.

He was also a stand-up guy, not prone to boasting about his experiences in the Falklands (which wouldn't have been the case with some of the other crew on board. Christ, we'd have never heard the end of it!). I remember him telling me there was no great feeling of jingoistic fervour on board

Conqueror, as was portrayed in the tabloids at the time of the sinking and which culminated in that appalling headline of 'GOTCHA' in the *Sun*. It was a simple case of doing the job that had been tasked of them. The time for reflection on what they'd done, the loss of life and the subsequent course of the war, came much later. As soon as the torpedoes had been launched they went into survival mode, with evasion the top priority in the depths of the South Atlantic. They hid away as skilfully and professionally as possible, with the sounds of torpedoes exploding and bulkheads caving in coming through the sonar as it recorded the whole event.

A lot of the crew from *Conqueror* subsequently enjoyed meteoric rises up the command structure of the Submarine Service. The captain went on to further commands and later retired as a holder of the Distinguished Service Order, the XO ended up a vice admiral after taking command of two more submarines and a stint as Teacher on Perisher training, while the navigator became the last captain of *Resolution* and then the first captain of *Victorious*, the Trident submarine.

Atkins made it clear what he expected of me in terms of the graft required to obtain my dolphins, and I was very thankful that I'd landed him as my corner man. Time stood still for me in many ways as I crammed in every minute I could, learning about the ship's systems that made the boat work, and as a new starter I didn't get the time to think or worry about why I'd opted for a life in what was essentially a cigar-shaped steel tube.

The main breakdown of submarine qualification splits into the following areas of acquired knowledge: submarine construction; knowledge of submarine operations; mechanical systems on board and ship systems on board; ordnance and sensor systems; electrical systems on board; nuclear reactor and associated propulsion systems; and a thorough knowledge of submarine escape. Learning about all of these would consume all my spare time during my first patrol, and my social life outside of watch-keeping was non-existent, as I wasn't allowed to watch any movies or films until I had my dolphins.

In some ways I suppose I felt isolated from the rest of the crew, but with their help I would get through it. It was expected that I'd learn the inner workings of the whole boat from forward to aft, a sort of naval equivalent of 'The Knowledge' for the drivers of London's black cabs. If there was a serious, life-threatening incident – such as a mechanical or hydraulic failure – and I was the closet person to it, I'd be expected to tackle it head on with a plan and not just stand there shitting bricks. It was all about being able to multitask and remain calm. Sounds easy on paper.

I had a Part 3 booklet covering the areas listed above, which I had to study and absorb one section at a time and then get tested on before I qualified. Whether it was learning about the engine room, the operation of the galley, how sonar or the reactor worked, cradling around looking for endless and never-ending fucking pipes, with both high pressure and low pressure running through them; learning about the high-pressure oil operation of hydraulics, how fresh water and oxygen were made, and how the sewage was pumped correctly, overboard instead of inboard; and, of course, my friends in the middle of the boat, the nuclear missiles.

The coxswain usually did the testing. 'Humph, you've passed,' he'd say, 'but only just. It was mainly bollocks.'

Standard praise, after I'd just explained to him how the foreplanes, afterplanes and rudder all worked when changing depth, course and speed.

One of the forward mechanics was 'Smudge' Smith, a hefty, tough and funny northerner with a voracious appetite. He took me under his wing and made it his aim to get me up to speed on all the mechanical systems forward of the missile compartment, as well as the firefighting procedures. Imagine your Uncle Dave at the bottom of the garden in his shed, mixed with a dash of Fred Dibnah, the chirpiness of Guy Martin and the drinking capacity of Oliver Reed. That was Smudge. Supremely barrel-chested and pot-bellied, he let it all hang out with his overalls barely fastened – big was beautiful, but he'd squeeze himself into the darkest recesses of the bilges no problem. There was nothing about how the mechanics of the boat worked that he didn't know. This was quite a slog for me as I was not at all mechanically gifted, but with Smudge's help I quickly got the hang of the essentials, overalls on, a stinking, sweaty mess down AMS 1,*

* Auxiliary machinery space.

looking at the main hydraulic plant and understanding its workings.

He also taught me the workings of the slop, drain and sewage tank, which was basically his responsibility. This tank dealt with collecting all the shit from the toilets and the waste from the galley sinks, which would first be cut up by a grinder (as the tank could only take waste in liquid form) known affectionately as Peter the Eater, then flushed into the tank by sea water. The tank was internal, which meant that if we were at depth there was too much water pressure for it to be evacuated correctly, so the boat had to be in shallower waters before it was pumped outboard. Otherwise it might vent inboard due to the adverse pressure; a total shit fest on 3 Deck, quite literally. There were occasions, however, when the pumping mechanisms weren't working correctly and the tank had to be blown out with compressed air. Fine in principle, but obviously a certain amount of pressure is required to blow the tank free of all the brown and smelly stuff – and this pressure remains in the tank after the shit has been evacuated. The pressure can't be vented outboard because large air bubbles rising to the surface might give the submarine's position away, so the only way to equalise it is to vent the air inboard through filters to remove any virulent gases. Imagine the stench of a 500-gallon sewage tank wafting through every inch of the sub. Think of something like a giant collective fart mixed with oil, body odour, rotten food, fags and booze and you're getting my drift. Slightly pungent.

Should operational conditions mean that we had to run deeper than normal for a certain period, the sewage tank would naturally become full but as we were too deep we couldn't use air pressure to blow it out. Also, if we were at a higher depth, the sound of blowing the shit tank overboard would have produced a noise signature that might give our position away, never mind any sea life that would burst into noisy complaint once they'd got a whiff. This led to the toilets not being flushed, which meant you were defecating onto someone else's shit; not something I recommend, particularly if the last person had threadworms. With three junior rates' toilets servicing around 80 men, the stench could quickly become intolerable, and it was all I could do to crap without retching. Sometimes it was so bad I would will myself to become constipated until the toilets were back online, usually 12 to 18 hours later. The senior rates' mess and wardroom also had toilets, but they enjoyed a much lower shit-to-number-of-toilets ratio; it was us hoi polloi who had the pleasure of seeing and then dumping on each other's poo.

The hours of grind and endless revision affected my ability to function on watch. After a couple of weeks on my first patrol I was having difficulty getting out of bed to go on duty. We were usually woken up 30 minutes before going on watch so we had time for a cup of tea, breakfast, dinner or lunch, depending on the time of day, real or perceived. I was so exhausted that I needed to be shaken at least two or three times before I even responded, and would turn up for watch late; a very bad thing at the best of times, but doing it as a Part 3 was a cardinal sin. By this stage I was at a total loss mentally and would wake up clueless as to where I was. Sleeping in pitch darkness, it normally takes time to adjust to natural light, but trying to adjust to artificial light was proving much more difficult. The solution to my sleepiness was that I was now to be woken up *an hour* before I went on watch and would have to relieve my counterpart 15 minutes early, which meant even less sleep and even less time to cram my studies in during my time off.

I was literally dragged from the top bunk in my sleeping bag, so I would be standing in it as if I were in the school sack race, blearily trying to work out who'd woken me up and where the fuck I was. Atkins, my mentor, let me know how it was. I wasn't to question him. It was sink – although not literally – or swim. At 18 years of age I experienced my first crisis of confidence; depressed but obviously unable to show it, it was the first time in my life I'd felt so isolated, worthless and stressed about the future.

Having these thoughts at many fathoms down was a struggle. I became introverted for a while and crawled into my shell as I struggled to cope with this newfound lack of resolve. Alone, unhappy, even frightened, my first time at sea was fast turning into a nightmare. Permanently knackered due to the work I was putting in off watch, coupled with the impact of the general living conditions – cramped, smelly, no privacy, only artificial light, recycled fresh air, temperature changes from very hot in the engineering spaces to quite cool in the control room – no wonder my young and fairly fit body was now a shambles. I'd had too much thrown at me and I simply couldn't cope.

Paranoia was also setting in. I thought I was receiving withering looks from crewmates everywhere I turned, whispered conversations about one of the new guys who couldn't get out of bed in time to go on watch … *The waster, he's not going to be able to hack it.* The paranoia became even more intense when, as I tucked into my breakfast one morning, I heard cries of 'Valentine, Valentine, will you be my Valentine?' This went on for about five minutes and I wondered what it was all about, then suddenly it became all too clear that the piss-take was being aimed at me by my own team. They'd been on watch overnight and had been looking through the crew's HR files – where everyone's full names were printed on top – with the duty officer of the watch. Of course, one of my middle names, Valentine, had been seen by the rest of the team and caused much merriment, and they were now ribbing me. It was said up into the air, though, never directly at me – classic traits of bullying – and it only happened at mealtimes and was never mentioned at any other time. I guess they felt happier in a bigger crowd.

Being the new guy, I could do nothing. I just had to take it. I started to dread watch-change mealtimes, as I knew they would be waiting for me, ready to start up all over again. Meals were supposed to be looked forward to, a time when the crew came together, but now I loathed the watch-change, the smug grins as they relieved me. It was bullying, no question – and they knew I could do nothing about it. People would have just laughed if I'd answered back.

I spoke to a couple of crewmates about it. One was extremely sympathetic and said I should go and talk to the coxswain about it, the other said I needed to 'grow a pair' and 'be a man' about it. Of course, that sounded ridiculous, suggesting that I couldn't talk through any problems and simply had to suffer in silence. Every time I hear someone say that modern phrase 'man up' these days, it just makes me want to punch them in the face.

In the end, the meal ritual went on for maybe two weeks and then suddenly stopped. I suppose my outward show of not being at all bothered finally had an effect, and without a response the barracking ceased. It had been a pretty awful situation, because there really was nowhere I could escape to apart from my bunk, and I had been spending less and less time there as my workload had steadily been increasing. I was in turmoil, given that I was a person who would usually tackle bullying head on, whether it happened to me or to someone else. The worse thing about it occurring at mealtimes was that I'd just come off watch and needed some relaxation, or I was about to go on watch so had to be alert and on point.

My childhood had been full of fights and scuffles, and I'd boxed both at school and at basic training, so I was certainly not going to shy away from physical confrontation if it came down to it. I was at loggerheads with my inner feelings, which were at boiling point – all I really wanted to do was stab my persecutors in the eye with a fork from the dinner table, but that was obviously out of the question. Yet I was stronger than them. I'd ignored them, and it had stopped.

This now felt equally weird, with the offenders chatting to me at watch changeover and at mealtimes as if nothing had ever happened. Perhaps it had been a test of character to see if I could hack life beneath the waves; it didn't feel much like a test at the time, more lonely and humiliating, to be quite frank. I think it boiled down to the fact that they were bored, didn't keep themselves occupied and thought taking the piss out of the new guy would pass the time. Pricks.

The episode taught me the importance of self-awareness, of being in control of one's actions. This was obviously key to life underwater – don't become rattled, learn to ignore those people you can't get on with and try to make the best of everything. The incident affected me more than it probably should have, but the group were a lot older than me, which makes it worse in hindsight, as they were experienced crew who ought to have been helping me to realise my potential, not intentionally making me feel miserable so I lost my confidence. It's a crucial fact of life anywhere, that there are always going to be people you don't get along with, but on board a submarine it's hugely magnified as it's so much harder to disappear and find solace and peace. Still, you have to try.

It wasn't just me who bore the brunt of this kind of behaviour. Others had to endure much worse, sometimes with tragic consequences. One leading mechanic arrived on a patrol later in my career with whip marks all down his back. He had a kinky private life, which was his business and his alone, but when someone saw the lacerations on his back, that was it. From then on he was ridiculed mercilessly, again under the protective auspices of banter. Shortly after arriving back from patrol he was found hanging from some sheets in the massive laundry shore-side. Who knows what led him to that terrible act, but the constant ridicule couldn't have helped.

Being different didn't make for an easy life under the sea. I learnt that if I was going to get along, I'd be the one who'd have to change and fit in with the rigours of military life. If it meant having to surrender some of my individuality to fit more into the team, then that's what I had to do.

About halfway through my first patrol I started to feel much more confident both within myself and with all the engineering systems I had to learn. I'd cracked the forward end of the boat, the coxswain signing it off with his usual praise: 'Humph, although that was a fucking disgrace, you've just passed.'

Now I was ready to take on the challenge of learning about the workings back aft; how the reactor worked, the propulsion, the steam generators. Time was flying by – busy, busy, busy. I literally did nothing but keep watch, then overalls and boots on back aft, back on watch, then back aft.

Nuclear submarines are wondrous machines. How difficult it must be to design a vessel that can stay submerged in the first place, added to which it must carry ballistic missiles as well as have the capacity to maintain life-support systems, food, oxygen (through the elimination of hydrogen and CO_2), plus a fully functioning nuclear reactor. What you're left with is a miracle of modern-day engineering, the equivalent, I suppose, of designing the Apollo spacecraft or the space shuttle.

The function of the nuclear reactor was simple, to produce as much heat as possible. It did this by generating steam to move the propeller and electricity to provide all the power the boat needed to function. The fuel used in the reactor was the highly radioactive material known as uranium, which can do great damage if not managed

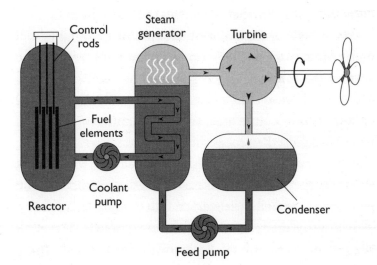

Nuclear reactor

correctly. The MEO and his team of elite engineers monitored this constantly throughout the patrol to keep the submarine and its crew safe.

When the reactor was flashed up for the first time a neutron was fired at a uranium atom – when it hit that atom it then split or fissioned, releasing energy and then freeing more neutrons. These neutrons continued the same actions of splitting when they hit the uranium atoms. This is known as a chain reaction and once it becomes self-supported the reactor is said to be critical, producing enormous amounts of heat.

The energy that the reactor gave off was used for one thing – to heat water. There were two circuits in the reactor that both passed water through a heat exchanger. One was at a very high pressure so it prevented the water from boiling, and one was at a much lower pressure that was boiling so it created steam. It was this steam that generated the power to control the turbines which provided all the capacity the submarine needed to function. Think of an old steam engine on a train, but replace the coal with uranium and the same principle holds; the process of heating water created steam, which drove the turbines that provided the submarine's power for the propeller, life systems (fresh-water and oxygen production) and all the electrical functions on board.

To control the reactor output control rods were used to regulate the amount of fission being generated. These control rods were made of elements such as hafnium and boron which, when immersed, soaked up energy and thus reduced the output of the reactor. Conversely, if they were gradually lifted from the reactor core the chain reaction would increase and so the power generated for production of steam would increase. If the reactor needed to be shut down for any reason, control rods would be fully lowered into the reactor, causing it to scram (shut down). A scram might occur for many reasons: a system failure, an error within the workings of the reactor itself, a stuck control rod or rods being removed too quickly when the reactor was being flashed up for the first time or restarted; or something more sinister that required an immediate shutdown, like a fire or a problem with a steam generator.

Given its size – the exact dimensions of the submarine's nuclear reactor were a secret, but its inner core was about as large as a wheelie bin – its power was incredible; the reactor could supply sufficient electricity to power a town the size of Swindon. Electricity was required on the boat not only to run its life-support systems, but also a wide range of other functions: the fridges and freezers that stored the food, the ovens and hot water for showers, washing and laundry, as well as maintaining the temperature on board. We had enough power to sail round the globe without stopping, and in theory could remain submerged for a few years, although murder and mayhem would have ensued after being cooped up for so long. Additionally, this extraordinary reactor also helped power what was then the best sonar equipment available, and the computers that armed and guided the most powerful weapon system Britain had ever produced.

Fission also produces radiation, so the reactor was lined with tonnes of lead shielding to keep the crew safe. It was a widely held view at the time that the Soviets' reactor shielding was insufficient, and that their reactors therefore posed a health and safety risk to the crews. In fact, some of the early Soviet nuclear boats emitted so much radiation that NATO considered trying to track them just by monitoring radiation levels in the oceans, a scary thought indeed. By the 1980s, however, the Soviet Navy under the stewardship of Admiral Gorshkov, a survivor of Stalin's purges of the military, had spent billions rebuilding their boats, increasing both their stealth and safety. The Soviets invested so much money on the arms race, around 15 to 20 per cent of GDP (to put that into perspective, the US in the last year of President Obama's tenure in 2016 spent around 3 per cent of GDP on defence, while the UK is committed to spending 2 per cent of GDP), that the people of the Soviet Union struggled to make ends meet and their declining living standards pushed them ever further away from the promises of the Politburo. The knock-on effect in the long term was that it helped to end the Cold War. This was a race communism could never win over the capitalist West; the money simply ran out, and to this day the former Soviet Union is still scattered with submarines left to rot in nuclear cesspits.

But I digress. The reactor and all of these associated systems were controlled by a crack team of engineers in the manoeuvring room. Led by the MEO, they basically ran a small power station under the sea. Having spent hours studying the reactor's workings, the next major subject that needed tackling was the workings of the purification equipment in AMS 2, how oxygen was made from the electrolysis of water, and the separation of CO_2 and hydrogen that made it possible.

In a submarine you need to look after life. As quickly as the oxygen is being spent, it must be renewed, because if oxygen levels fall sufficiently low, everyone will suffocate. Meanwhile, CO_2 must be expelled from the environment before it turns into poison, and should the CO_2 levels rise above 1 per cent it could be risky for the crew on board. So CO_2 was removed by 'scrubbers' that were on the go 24/7 to get it out of the atmosphere and pumped overboard to keep everything ticking over in maintaining life-support systems.

Seawater is used to make oxygen through the process of electrolysis, whereby water is pumped on board, then purified through the purification plant, after which an electrical charge is passed through it by electricity generated from the nuclear reactor. With the application of electricity, the water is split into its two main component parts, oxygen and hydrogen. The hydrogen is liquefied before being pumped overboard (as it can become explosive if mixed with the oxygen), while all that lovely oxygen is passed through the ventilation systems so the crew can breathe. Each member of the crew needed between 10 to 15 cubic metres of air every day, just to stay alive. The oxygen levels weren't as high as in your average house or office block, however;

oxygen can be a killer in the enclosed space of a submerged submarine, as it can feed a small fire to the extent that it rapidly grows and gets out of control.

It was also here in AMS 2 that I got into weight-training to keep fit. Andy, a Scot and one of the back aft mechanics, had bought some weights with him, so I used to hang out there a lot, learning about various purification principles and boffing up on reactor knowledge, followed by a workout of rip curls and bench presses, as well as chin-ups on carefully selected pipes. It broke up the monotony of the day, plus there was only one exercise bike for a crew of 143.

Six weeks into my first patrol I felt sufficiently ready for the exam to get my dolphins and become a fully fledged member of the service. I remember feeling very nervous as I made my way up to the torpedo compartment for the oral exam. Sitting there were the coxswain, the chief engineer, whom I got on well with, and the XO, a stickler for detail. He'd had a long and distinguished career, had captained two diesel submarines and would go on to command two of the Polaris boats before they were decommissioned.

The atmosphere was tense. I began by drawing a basic outline of the nuclear reactor and how it created the steam that ultimately drove the propeller shaft and moved the sub. Next up, I explained the so-called 'fleeting' procedure required during a rush escape, and how the boat surfaced and dived. Nearly two hours in and I feared the worst, as the XO – who had already failed three people that week, and whose examinations were legendary – was asking particularly searching questions that I was struggling to answer. After I'd been in there for three hours he asked for a drawing of the auxiliary vent-and-blow system, which I'd not fully revised, and then he got up and marched out. The coxswain informed me later that I hadn't failed, but the exam had gone on so long that everyone – most of all me – needed a break. We'd reconvene at a later date.

There was only a week to go until the end of patrol, so I was now in limbo, the XO being busy with mess dinners, so I kept up the revision not knowing when I'd get the bloody thing finished. A week went quickly by and we were then back in port, alongside. The following day I was summoned to a room shore-side to continue the exam. Here I found the navigator on his own waiting for me. He asked me a couple of fairly simple questions, to which I rattled off the answers, and the next minute he was giving me a box with dolphins inside. I'd passed, albeit in fairly bizarre style. I didn't care, though, as I'd joined the club now. I would do the traditional presentation next time I was at sea, which consisted of drinking a glass of rum with the dolphins in it. This I did and caught the dolphins in my teeth, which were then pinned onto my suit. Off I fucked.

12

ALL THE TIME IN THE WORLD

Once I'd become a qualified submariner with more free time on my hands, the issue of managing time became much more pressing. The endless bustling around the boat I'd done, looking for hull valves, switches, absorption units and electrolysers, was now over. While life was easier on the one hand, I now had to make my own entertainment off watch, and cope with the inevitable downtime and boredom.

Education was one sure-fire way to eliminate ennui. I always tried to picture a life outside of the service, so enrolled myself on two A-level correspondence courses: one in law, the other in government and politics. Also, the new navigator on board was running O-level navigation classes, and since my day job centred on elements of navigation, it seemed like a sensible idea to join these. I'd purchased the set textbooks before patrol and cracked on while at sea, spending at least two hours every day studying, usually stuck away in the sonar console space, which tended to be one of the quietest areas for work and contemplation. I soon understood why many long-term prisoners gained further education qualifications and degrees. It's not just that they can work as much or as little as they like, more that conditions when confined are perfect for studying; that, and the availability of time. It was the same on a sub.

In my later working life I met convicted armed robber John McVicar, who'd also done A-level courses while in jail in the early 1970s. In addition, he'd completed a sociology degree. By then he'd become a journalist, and he talked about the need for constant self-improvement to better his life and situation. This, to me, was what my studying was all about. I'd done OK with my O-levels, but nothing to write home about. I hated a lot of the subjects and just scraped by in most of them with the minimum amount of effort. I'd been too much involved in extra-curricular activities, most notably girls, music and drink. But studying for A-levels on the sub was a different matter altogether, as I was very interested in the law and fascinated by political discourse.

I soon got used to the gentle hum of the air cooling the sonar gear as I studied family and common law, legislation, proportional representation, the history of the labour movement and the constitution of the Unites States. Those days were of course pre-email, pre-computers even, so I would be doing two or three months' worth of work and then sending it all off to get marked once I'd returned from patrol. As a result the courses dragged on a little, but it was worth it because when I left the service I secured a place at university in London to read history.

I suppose I was an outsider, perhaps a tad different compared with the other junior rates on board. I'd started out my career looking for something to test and intrigue me. But as soon as I'd got my dolphins, my head was already being turned by thoughts of what I'd do later in life. Education felt like it would open opportunities for me after I was done with the Silent Service, and reading about law and politics proved more interesting than the readers wives' pages of *Razzle*. Mind you, we all needed that on occasion.

That's not to say that I didn't get on well with most people on board, apart from the bullying incident on my first patrol. Studying helped break the day up into a manageable routine and took my mind off the constant thoughts of potential danger, which living in a steel coffin could certainly provoke. While it helped me switch off from the stresses and strains of everyday underwater life, I also found the education process stimulating. If I hadn't enrolled in study, I'm not sure how I'd have coped with the inevitable long periods of boredom and isolation off watch. It was easy to sink into a zombie-like state of sleep, eat, drink, shit and repeat.

But the most important part of being able to study was the solitude it gave me. Even at the best of times, other people can be very annoying – myself included; but under the sea, with the knowledge that there's nowhere to escape, people can drive you fucking crazy. In the space of 30 seconds a friendly chat with someone might easily turn into a nasty, full-blown row. Sometimes you simply needed to vent, and it would usually be the nearest person in the firing line who copped your wrath. It was never personal – well, very rarely – just a product of the conditions we had to put up with. Being out of other people's faces studying meant I was usually greeted by most people like some long-lost relative, and relaxation time was chilled and passed without incident – just how it should have been. People constantly on edge and on the look-out for arguments were simply not suited to the service. If there's one thing a submariner needs above all else, it's a sensible disposition and the ability to live and let live. Studying helped me remain sane.

Sometimes I'd just sit in the sonar console space thinking about what was out in front of us, outside the sub. I'd get a rising feeling of doom in my gut that the sonar hadn't picked something up and we were going to hit it full-on; that it would come straight through the pressure hull and I'd be sucked out into the depths of the ocean below. This was not as far-fetched as it seemed, as *Resolution* travelled so slowly that it hardly gave off any acoustic signature. This, coupled with its covering of anechoic tiles, made us almost unde-tectable. And, if another submarine, whether it be French, Russian or American, was in the same area, then who knows? An underwater collision was certainly possible.

It wasn't all work, though. Physical exercise played a key role in keeping up some of the crew's morale throughout the patrol. There was a keep-fit class twice a week run by one of the chief wreckers. He was an early adopter of the triathlon and spent most of his spare time off the boat competing in events up and down the country, but given that it was the mid- to late-80s, I'd never heard of the sport before. Needless to say, his keep-fit classes were pretty hard core. At the age of 19 I considered myself reasonably fit, but after an hour of sit-ups, press-ups, burpees, squat thrusts and shadow-boxing, I was ready to puke.

The oxygen and ventilation used to get cranked up both during and after exercise to help us breathe better, and also to clear the collective stench of ten sweaty submariners after an hour's workout. The oxygen supply was controlled by the MEO, and he would turn it up if he wanted people doing lots of work and turn it down if he wanted people to be quiet.

After exercise, all I wanted to do was have a nice, long shower, but in our world of conserving water, this just wasn't going to happen. The rule about showering in a submarine was simple: use the least amount of water possible. So I'd turn on the shower for 10 to 15 seconds until my hair and body were wet, then switch it off, wash said hair and body thoroughly, then switch the water back on and rinse for 30 seconds – max. A full shower in under a minute. Woe betide anyone who took longer than that. There'd be hell to pay if you were accused of having a 'Hollywood' or 'hotel' shower, and it would be a long time before you next got to wash from head to toe. Don't imagine there was any privacy either, for there was no shower curtain. I'd be standing there stark bollock naked having a chat with someone shaving in one of the sinks next to the showers, while someone else was laying cable in trap three, with fruity sound effects.

Private time it definitely wasn't. If we had to conserve water or couldn't use the showers because we were running in quiet state due to a perceived threat in the area, I had to resort to a single sink of water, with which I was expected to have an all-over wash using a flannel, a teeth-clean and a shave – assuming I wasn't growing a beard.

Talking of beards, they've been allowed in the Navy for hundreds of years. Not moustaches, mind; we leave those for the Army and RAF. Beards were common on patrol, if in a minority. I wish I could say mine lived up to expectations, but I was no Herman Melville. Trying to grow one at such a young age was difficult. I looked like someone had stuck some pubic hair on various parts of my face, and if I'd gone up top when we'd surfaced, a gust of wind would have blown the lot off. It was useful to do, though, as it prevented unnecessary water use. My beard-growing skills have improved considerably with age and I have a full, lustrously thick one now that would have been deemed too long back on *Resolution*.

As I've mentioned, there was an exercise bike in the missile compartment that was in constant demand throughout the day, so the best time to use it was in the middle of the night. I'd sit on it listening to Kraftwerk's 'Tour de France' on my Walkman, imagining I was Greg LeMond powering up the 21 hairpins of Alpe d'Huez. The bike was a great conduit for de-stressing from the daily grind of patrol, and further into my career a rowing machine was introduced, which led to competitions as to who could row the furthest on the metres gauge in five minutes. These informal events were probably the closest to death I've ever come.

In the lower level of the torpedo compartment, usually late at night if I was off watch, I used to shadowbox to keep trim. I'd do it for two minutes at a time, for around ten to twelve minutes. It was surreal because I was usually in darkness and almost total silence, and the only sound I could hear was my own breathlessness, sweat sluicing off me as I threw uppercuts, hooks and jabs, my feet bouncing off the compartment floor as I weaved in and out of the torpedo racks firing off salvos of punches at the tubes themselves. It totally immersed me, narrowed my focus, and was perhaps the closest to meditation I could get. A warm glow would come over me as I caught my second wind, and for that ten minutes or so I could have been anywhere in the world.

13

DOWNTIME

We had a weekly ship's quiz on board, in many ways like a *University Challenge*-type quiz night. The competition would take place most weeks of the patrol, culminating in a grand final, and most departments would send out one or two teams and we'd have a full-blown tournament – yet another thing to break up the monotony of the day-to-day grind. Buzzers were rigged up by the WEMs to get the proper TV vibe when answering, and the doctor hosted, pretending to be Bamber Gascoigne, the only resemblance being that they both spoke the English language. These quizzes were serious stuff, with full-on revision the day before, sitting in front of an encyclopaedia trying to memorise capital cities, world affairs and all the rest.

I got the nod to be in one of the teams on my first patrol, mainly due to the fact that I'd been able to name every British PM in the correct order from the beginning of the 20th century when they were picking the teams.

Even the captain put in an appearance at the quarter-final, where my warfare and sonar team had been battling back and forth with a bunch of sweaty engineers. The tiebreak question came up: 'What was the major change in voting law that happened in the Representation of the People Act 1969?' Quick as a flash I buzzed in and answered, 'It meant that all people between 18 and 20 now got the vote, as well as the existing voters over 21, though you couldn't stand for parliament unless you were 21.' The skipper looked visibly excited and probably couldn't believe a junior rating like myself would be capable of such an answer. 'Well done, well done!' he kept saying.

On a subsequent patrol my team made it through to the final but were pipped at the post by a team of engineering officers. There seemed to be an inordinate number of questions on physics and chemistry, so us non-mechanical types from the front end stood no chance. The fix was in.

Usually at around half to three-quarters of the way into the patrol we had the horse-racing night, when departments would enter their very own self-made horse, usually made out of papier-mâché. Some looked great, with real care having gone into their construction, while others were reminiscent of my youngest son's craft classes at nursery. I was the bookie's mate on a number of these occasions, and one of our senior leading hands in the tactical systems department was the son of a fairly successful Edinburgh bookie, so he was very adept at 'dealing' with the large amounts of money that swam around on these booze-fuelled nights. A percentage of the profits always went to charity, but even so it could end with a few quid made here and there. Six horses would be auctioned off to the highest bidder. Why six? It was all dice related, so there were six horses in six separate lanes, fences also included. The dice were thrown, the first one to see which horse moved, the second one to see how many spaces it moved, which led to much wailing and gnashing of teeth if you lost money, but smiles and a few beers all round if your horse romped in. Those with hangovers often woke up the next day thinking about how much their gambling would cost them when they got back alongside to settle their bar bills.

14

BOOZE

Napoleon once said, 'An army marches on its stomach. To be effective, an army relies on good and plentiful food.' While that may have been all well and good for our camouflaged Action Man friends, the Royal Navy has a history of being a well-oiled war machine fuelled on liquor.

As far back as the 1700s the Navy began a rum ration to men serving in the West Indies, which consisted of a half-pint neat ration daily – sounds great. By the 1740s, however, the ration was being diluted with water and became known as 'grog', a term for rum and lime (or lemon juice), the latter added to help prevent scurvy. This daily ration lasted in one form or another until 1970, when it was finally phased out due to the complexity of modern equipment and heavy machinery, which wasn't really tailored to being operated by sailors who'd stand no chance at a breathalyser test.

The culture of drinking drifted steadily away from the tot of rum and switched to beer. This occurred throughout all branches of the service, from 'skimmers' – surface ships – to the magnificent men, and now women, of the Submarine Service. You might think that being on a nuclear submarine, and in my case, on the nuclear deterrent, would warrant a ban on the hard stuff and an insistence on temperance for patrol cycles – but not one jot of it. Thank God! We were allowed to drink up to three cans of beer per day as junior rates, with senior rates and officers around the same, although they also had access to beer on draught. There was a bar in the senior rates' mess where pints would be served and stewards would carry them down 2 Deck to the wardroom. So, given that a crew of 143 men could drink roughly the equivalent of three cans per day for an average patrol length of, say, 60 days, that was a lot of beer – both kegs and cans – to load up. There were roughly 75 junior rates on board, so that's over 10,000 cans of booze right there. Of course, not everyone would imbibe their allocated lot – and that's where the fun began. If I'd drunk my three cans and my ship mate didn't want to drink that day, he'd sign them out under his name and give them to me, or vice versa.

This could lead to a situation where, of an evening, some of the crew and I could easily be drinking at least nine to twelve cans of beer each. On every third day the watch system rotated, so when I finished my watch at 8 p.m. and was not required until 8 the following morning, that was the time to indulge. We'd regularly work through crates of cans on those nights, and I suppose we saw it as a release from it all to enjoy the comforts of life at home for a few hours. I've been fortunate enough to have fairly good sea legs in terms of alcohol consumption; others, however, were not so blessed.

One night I'd just finished showing a film in the junior rates' mess, I think it was *The Untouchables* with Kevin Costner and Sean Connery. Seated to my right was one of the chefs. For most of the evening he'd been enjoying plenty of canned lager, getting steadily more and more soused as each hour went by, and he continued to drink after the film, finally getting up shakily to leave. We all thought he'd gone to the toilets, and who knows, that might have been his original intention, but in fact he'd ended up somewhere else altogether. Suddenly, shouting and swearing erupted from the 3 Deck sleeping quarters. It sounded like there was a huge punch-up on its way. It turned out that instead of going to the toilets, he'd entered the chefs' and stewards' sleeping quarters, pulled back the curtain on his off-duty chef buddy and proceeded to piss all over him. Of course, I don't need to say that we hushed up the whole incident to save him from some huge bollocking in front of the XO, or indeed face the captain's table.

On another occasion, one of the stewards on board had drunk himself into oblivion in the torpedo compartment, which doubled up as the junior rates' mess deck. He attempted to make his way to the toilets, and while traversing through a watertight bulkhead, slipped and fell through the fridge space hatch onto the floor below. It had been left open as one of the chefs was finding ingredients to prep breakfast the next morning. About wide enough to get a man through, it's remarkable he didn't kill himself by clipping his chin on the steel hatch and pushing his jawbone up into his brain as he fell through it. At the time, we thought we might be storing our first body in the refrigeration space. Remarkably, he climbed out of the deceptively cold compartment as if nothing had happened, then bounced off the walls as he quick-stepped his way to the toilet.

Looking back, I shudder at the thought of what might have happened if we'd had a sudden catastrophic emergency to deal with, with me, and indeed others, laid up in the torpedo compartment considerably the worse for wear. Not cool. For all the boozing though, I never once went on duty drunk, nor did any of my crew mates. Yes we played hard, but it was game face on come watch time. But social time on board *Resolution* centred upon alcohol consumption. It was good for the nerves, chilled out most people and led to an easier life; hardly ever was it a catalyst for violence or a row.

For me and many of the crew, alcohol was essential to break up the monotony of patrol life. I mean, what are you meant to do, cooped up deep in the ocean? There were no PlayStations in each mess, no internet access, no chance to send emails. We couldn't be expected to live like monks; we needed a release, a sense of freedom, even for a few precious hours. And besides, it kept spirits up. Admittedly, some people, including myself, were fairly infantile in their approach to drinking at sea. Most sailors drink to get pissed, whether at sea or ashore, and we certainly drank ourselves to near oblivion shore-side. On many a morning I woke up in my shared dorm on shore, not knowing how I'd got back from wherever I'd been the previous night – a nightclub, restaurant or a girl's flat.

It was the same at sea. I was young and impressionable, and there was considerable peer pressure to knock back a few 'tinnies'. When you're two to three hundred feet below the North Atlantic, you've only just passed Day 2 of 90 and have finished your watch in the control room, you kind of need the fix. If alcohol hadn't been permitted, a lot of the crew would have gone stir crazy, as surviving on a social life of uckers and other board games was not going to cut the mustard. The great thing, though, was that if there was any trouble, such as the incidents I alluded to earlier, it was all kept in mess, for what happened in the junior rates' mess very much stayed in the junior rates' mess; no snitching to senior rates or officers, with the experienced leading hands keeping everything in line without going over the top. And it was good to be treated as an adult, which I was, just about ...*

---

* Drinking has rightly been heavily curtailed since the tragic death of Lt Cdr Ian Molyneux in 2011, when he was murdered on board the nuclear submarine HMS *Astute* while heroically defending the rest of the crew by selflessly putting himself between crazed gunman Able Seaman Ryan Donovan and fellow shipmates. Donovan had been allowed to handle a weapon, even though he had drunk more than 20 pints of cider and lager, as well as vodka and cocktails in the 48 hours before his attack. The Navy now enforces similar levels to the UK drink-driving laws, and even lower for personnel handling weapons.

15

SNADGENS

There was also a laissez-faire attitude towards smoking. The whole of the junior rates' mess was awash with smokers – on many nights the stratosphere of smoke in there resembled the Coach and Horses pub in Soho circa the late 1970s, where the clouds of tobacco were lit up by artificial lights. The junior rates' dining hall, which doubled up as the cinema most evenings, was quite literally befogged as you squinted to see the film through a thick haze of smoke. You could also grab a cheeky smoke in the senior rates' mess, the wardroom and some of the engineering spaces back aft. Thank God it was not permitted in any of the sleeping areas, as I'm not sure I would have got any sleep, anxious that the fire alarm would go off as someone torched themselves in their bunk.

I loved the odd cheroot – a thin brown cigar – usually after dinner with a beer while watching a movie. I think it was my teenage obsession with Clint Eastwood in Sergio Leone's spaghetti westerns that had prompted me to smoke them. I even invested in a poncho I'd found on a visit to

Camden Lock market. I'd wear it some nights if I was showing a western; I must have looked a right tart. I was never a huge fan of puffing away, but I'd say that at least 30 to 40 per cent of the boat were smokers. Again, like boozing, smoking was regarded by the crew as a means of psychological escape from the grind of patrol, a relaxant, and the prospect of a nicotine addict going cold turkey while submerged somewhere under a vast expanse of ocean didn't warrant thinking about. It was also a routine, something of paramount importance on patrol. I'd regularly see the same people having a black coffee and a couple of ciggies before they went on watch; it was the little things that got you through. One sonar leading hand who'd served about 16 years in subs told me he'd had a fried breakfast – when available – every day of his career, followed by three Marlboro reds. Then and only then would he be ready to go on watch. His skin had a deathly pallor to it; he resembled a living corpse – just like the character Johann in *Das Boot* – and was nicknamed 'The Ghost'. I hope he's enjoying a long and happy retirement now, but I have my doubts.

The worst part about smoking was the stink that it left on your clothes. Mine used to smell rank after about half an hour when I was showing a movie in the junior rates' canteen, whether I was smoking or not. I started taking three extra shirts on patrol to stave off the whiff. Cigarettes were readily available for purchase from the canteen, 200 fags a time, all the popular brands. It was like shopping in the duty free of an airport, but in this case with neither flight nor holiday to look forward to. Nicotine stains on bulkheads and walls had to be removed when cleaning the boat ('scrubbing out' it was called), but thank Christ I never had to do those particular areas – buckets full of black water as tar from the fag smoke was removed, and many a submariner gagging while doing it.

16

PORN

I'd not come across much pornography before I joined submarines, as it was absent from basic training and submarine school. As a teenager, there were the obligatory magazines like *Fiesta* or *Penthouse* I looked at with school friends, the normal exposure of a spotty, clueless and ill-informed adolescent. This was to change as soon as I joined submarines, for what did 143 men do while away at sea? Watch porn films, lots of them, most nights … well, every night.

My first encounter was almost immediately after diving on my first patrol. I was in the torpedo compartment being shown how the torpedoes were loaded and fired, and making copious notes, but all I could hear coming from upstairs was the funky soundtrack of a 1970s porn film accompanied by the muffled cries of the two main protagonists. On climbing to the upper level where I'd be learning about the life-support equipment on board – oxygen generators, absorption units, candles and the escape tower – out of the corner of my eye I spotted a wild-eyed, long-haired, moustachioed American man (John Holmes, apparently) and a voluptuous woman having intercourse in a very noisy manner until they reached the customary climax.

I found myself red-faced and mumbling apologies as I stumbled around, mortified, having inadvertently gate-crashed the porno film. I couldn't imagine anything worse than sitting around with 12 sweaty blokes in overalls and hard-ons, but as a newbie I had to shut my mouth and deal with it. There was nothing more distracting than trying to learn about the everyday system dynamics of a ballistic missile-carrying submarine while some pornstar in the background grunted his way towards orgasm. Besides, as a Part 3 trainee I wasn't allowed to watch any films at all, be they *Blue Velvet*, *Stand by Me* or *Debbie Does Dallas*.

After qualifying, if anything it made matters worse, as I was then expected to sit up watching porn half the night with fellow shipmates. I've never been one for sharing sexual intimacies unless with loved ones, and this just seemed bonkers, all of us staring at something that was simply unattainable under the ocean. If anything, it just made everything worse, at least for me; the last thing I needed to be thinking about all the time was sex. It was enough to make a sane man weep, sitting around one of the tables in the rec space with a collective hard-on in complete silence apart from the panting on the TV or someone shouting at new trainees to 'Get the fuck out of the way!' It was incessant, and gave me a good reason to find something better to do when off watch, being one of the main factors that drove me to study for A-levels.

The officers turned a blind eye to the porn. They used to come up to the mess when it was on and hang around watching it, until they received a menacing look from the older experienced junior rates and then slid away. The boat had its resident porn baron, who used to spend most of his off-crew time in Amsterdam, nosing round for the latest trends and returning with armfuls of the latest European and American hard-core action. He also passed round Polaroids of 'friends' in various stages of undress. Pure class.

Porn was rife. It was available 24/7, whether you liked it or not, and was symptomatic of the Navy at the time. The sex and drinking culture ruled, and if you weren't prepared to follow it you were singled out and mercilessly teased. It was never that bad for me, as I bowed to peer pressure, but I succeeded in avoiding the harder stuff. Of course, the seasoned porn watchers would be straight onto you if they thought you weren't one of them.

'I'm off to read *Moby Dick*,' I said one night.

'*Moby Dick?* You've got all the dick you need here, son,' came the reply.

I wanted Scotty to beam me up. I guess porn was inadvertently seen as a bonding experience; watching something outrageous and taboo in a group makes it a shared secret from the rest of the world. With everyone in such close proximity I suppose it reinforced everyone's perceived but ever-so-slightly warped view of heterosexuality.

We could also watch other videos in the rec space, of the conventional movie kind. A particular favourite of mine, and indeed the rest of the crew, was Wolfgang Petersen's epic *Das Boot*. This followed the crew of the German *U-96* through the narration of Lt Werner, who has been assigned to the crew as a war correspondent. The boat's captain, Lehmann-Willenbrock, played by Jürgen Prochnow, is a chiselled, battle-hardened sea dog. Very much the anti-Nazi, he holds any staunch believers in complete contempt as he battles the Atlantic, the Straits of Gibraltar, the Royal Navy and the brutal conditions on board, to survive with a very young crew. A certain degree of narcissism led us to put it on time and again, especially for the near disasters where the boat is depth-charged and sinks to the bottom of the sea, and watching this under the sea ourselves, we'd sit in silence thanking the Almighty nothing like that had happened to us.

17

FAMILYGRAMS

While at sea there was no communication from us to the outside world for the duration of the patrol, unless there was a catastrophic failure that would leave the submarine in peril, or perhaps a serious illness or injury on board that required better surgical procedures than were available to us. I'm not sure the boat could have handled surgery of any but the most basic kind; it would have been akin to performing an operation in a dank, dark basement of a seedy Shoreditch pub.

Once a week I was able to receive a familygram from my nominated next of kin, my father, telling me what was going on in the outside world. Like all our other communications these family missives came via Submarine Command in Northwood, and they could be no longer than 40 words. Nor could they contain any bad news, as this would be weeded out before transmission when they were checked and probably read by the radio operators, and then by the captain, so I'd be reading them third-hand. Dad usually kept it pretty formal, as he was aware the familygrams were scrutinised before being sent and were read by others at the receiving end. His messages were all run-of-the-mill stuff about what he and the family had been up to, peppered with the latest world news and sports results. He was able to pack a surprising amount of information into 40 words. These missives were in many ways a lifesaver, for they gave me a sense that someone outside of the boat cared about my welfare. I suppose in many ways they stopped me from cracking up – receiving conversation, albeit one-way, from family who had put some thought into what they were writing. The arrival of the familygram was something to look forward to, and the day they arrived everybody would feel more upbeat knowing they were a week closer to being back alongside in Faslane.

Some people needed familygrams more than others; the married men on board, for instance, were on tenterhooks every week for the next message from the wife and kids. It was the big moment of the week for them, and many used to carry the message around for a couple of days, re-reading it at regular intervals. Even catastrophically bad news was kept from the crew member concerned, until the submarine was close to coming back to port. There were deaths in the family on some of my patrols, involving parents and close family members. The fact that such tragic news was withheld illustrated the seriousness of the times, for deterrent patrols stopped for no one – it wasn't a game, and we were effectively in a state of war. So the captain had to deal with bad news as best as he saw fit, but it wasn't in any way going to upset the patrol cycle. The crew member wouldn't be airlifted off; he wouldn't be told what had happened until he'd nearly made it home to what he thought was going to be a happy reunion.

18

SHOWTIME

The doctor on board was not only responsible for treating ill sailors and hosting our quiz competitions. One of his other main duties, and probably the most important of the lot, was to choose approximately 55 films before patrol to take to sea with us for film nights. The films would go on around an hour or so after evening dinner and were looked forward to immensely as a relaxing way to round off the day. From my second patrol onwards – after I'd earned my dolphins – I became one of the projectionists who presented the evening movie. We'd take it in turns, so I'd probably show a film once every three or four days.

Maybe it had something to do with our 'special relationship' with the Americans, but somehow we managed to get our hands on the latest Hollywood releases, and indeed many that hadn't yet been released. The films would be on spoon reels that I fitted onto the projector like an old-fashioned cine reel. The junior rates' dining hall would be cleared after dinner, a pull-down screen placed in front of the adjoining senior rates' bar and a curtain was pulled across to block out the light from the galley where the chefs would be prepping for the following morning's breakfast or baking bread and cakes.

I'd always take care when removing the spools from their cases and attaching them to the projector that I'd got them the right way round – it was never a great move to switch off all the lights, roll the film and then discover I was showing it upside down. Once the spools were successfully loaded it was lights out all round, and as I switched on the projector we'd forget all about the soulless depths of the ocean pressing in on us just a few feet away, and escape into the film for the next two hours or so, be it Tom Cruise in *Top Gun*, Harrison Ford in *Witness*, Jodie Foster in *The Accused* or Robin Williams in *Good Morning, Vietnam* and *Dead Poets Society*. The list was endless, the films usually at the mass-appeal end of the spectrum, as naturally they were chosen to suit most tastes on board. This wasn't the place to start showing *Jean de Florette* or *Au revoir les enfants*, but I did, however, enjoy showing semi-cult classics such as David Lynch's *Blue Velvet*, William Friedkin's *To Live and Die in L.A.*, John Carpenter's *Big Trouble in Little China* and Alex Cox's *Repo Man*. These nights at the movies were the single biggest escape from the monotony of patrol and the humdrum of daily life. At no time in my entire life, before or since, did I derive as much joy from the cinema as during my days under the sea.

It was weird to think that back in the real world people would be off to the local Odeon to watch the same films we were viewing in a location unknown. We might not have had popcorn, but I had my beers and cheroots. These two-hour movie nights offered me a chance to let out emotions that no one else could see in the dark; alone with my thoughts in the make-believe world of celluloid, I could have a little cry or a laugh behind my projector in complete privacy, as it was so noisy with the volume of the film.

I distinctly remember being reduced to a blubbering wreck when I watched Sean Connery's death scene in *The Untouchables* for the first time, with De Palma's expert use of the camera as Connery crawls across the floor, blood pooling from an assassin's gun wound and '*Vesti la giubba*' from the opera *Pagliacci* being sung in the background. It was riveting. I loved the film nights, the beauty of cinema, and how it transported me to a different time and place. That was the important bit. It meant I could dream of else-where, escape the present and think about the future, all of which were crucial to maintain a sense of myself in this faraway, isolated world I now occupied. The movies could keep me going for three to four days until it was time to show another one; then, when the film ended, I'd be back to square one, the lights on, reality returning with a harsh bump as I rewound the spool and packed up the projector ready for the next showing. Dreams over, bed following soon after.

At the end of each patrol, a theatrical performance – or 'sod's opera', as it was known throughout the service – was put on by the ship's company. This invariably involved a mixture of comedy (with a small 'c') and music, with sailors dressed-up in drag, sporting fake boobs and tutus – a truly harrowing sight. The night would be compered by one of the senior CPOs, who would turn the air blue with a string of jokes that would have made even Bernard Manning wince; an acquired taste, perhaps. In between the awful jokes, however, there'd be some good piss-takes of crew-mates, several musical performances, usually acoustic guitars, baking competitions and the aforementioned cross-dressing in women's lingerie.

19

UNDER THE LIGHTS

Qualifying for my dolphins had been a sobering experience, with such a volume of work and study required that I didn't have much time to think about being shut off from the world. I'd been so busy that time had simply flown by, and the patrol was over before I had the chance to fully get to grips with my newfound life. Subsequent patrols, however, brought home just how difficult everyday life aboard a submarine really was. Scientists, and indeed many military types themselves, have noted the similarities between astronauts and submariners: how we both live in conditions of confinement, follow rigorous daily procedures and live on recycled air. There is also, of course, limited physical space in both environments, together with a lack of choice as to whom the sailors and astronauts work alongside, thrust together as they are with people whose company they're obliged to keep, whether they like them or not.

One key difference is that in space you can enjoy euphoric vistas of our magnificent planet that live long in the memory; whereas on a sub you spend ten to twelve weeks in the absolute darkness of the ocean, not knowing from the minute you dive to the moment the boat breaks the water and surfaces some three months later where the hell you've been. And, on occasion, it does feel like hell.

The first challenge of life on a submarine that becomes immediately apparent is the lack of any natural light. Imagine spending up to three months solid without looking at the sky, sun, moon and stars. No getting up and pulling open the curtains to admire a beautiful summer or winter's day; here we were, locked away, with only fluorescent lighting guiding our way. Among the chief disadvantages of having no natural light is that it leads to a drop in vitamin D levels. Vitamin D is essential for maintaining a number of health functions that serve the body both physiologically and behaviourally. Maintaining calcium in the bones through exposure to sunlight and ultra-violet radiation is vital; people can be susceptible to rickets if the level of exposure drops, which, if left unchecked, can cause weak and soft bones, skeletal deformity and, in some extreme cases, stunted growth. The effect of the lack of natural light on our circadian rhythms is also pronounced, and there's now clear evidence that the light-sensitive membranes in the rods and cones of the eye suffer from its absence too.

Of course, at the tender age of 18 I had no idea about any of this, and it was never discussed with my fellow sailors. Nowadays, I believe submariners aboard the nuclear deterrent receive vitamin D tablets to compensate for any drop in levels. To this day I regularly take supplements as I'm low in vitamin D on account of the months and years spent under the oceans.

Of most interest, perhaps, are the reports that light affects various behaviours, including levels of activity and aggression, and eating and drinking habits. An absence of natural light can make for seriously pissed-off people. Most living organisms, and I include submariners here, are subject to circadian rhythms; evolved over millions of years, these are the behavioural and physiological systems that keep the body in tune with the alternation of day and night. Circadian rhythms include sleep–wake cycles, as human beings are active during the day (diurnal) and sleep at night. Our body clocks are synchronised to the rising and setting of the sun, and if you start messing with natural light the body starts to function erratically, be it testosterone levels, metabolic processes or the quality of sleep.

Circadian rhythms are regulated and controlled by a part of the brain called the hypothalamus, which is connected to the optic nerves that respond to natural light, thus acting as the body's master clock and governing performance of our internal systems throughout the day. So when the sun comes up and the optic nerves first sense light coming through to the brain, the hypothalamus sends a signal to the body to raise our heartbeat and increase our blood pressure, and, as it assumes we're about to become active, it stops releasing sleep-inducing hormones such as melatonin, and so our alertness increases.

Performance-wise, we tend to be at our peak in the late morning, followed by a lull just after lunch, when our need for sleep is second only to that period in the early hours of the morning between say 1 to 4 a.m. In the evening, the optic nerves in the brain sense the disappearing daylight and our organs start to wind down, our temperature drops and sleep-inducing hormones are released, this being the final stage of the whole 24-hour cycle. Interestingly, no other species exhibits the same once-a-day sleeping pattern that humans have become accustomed to.

Recently it's been discovered that people with unusual lifestyle patterns that disrupt their natural circadian rhythm cycle have a greater propensity for obesity, depression, dementia, reproductive problems, heart disease and diabetes. It's also believed that up to 15 per cent of our genes may be regulated by circadian rhythms. Being on a submarine, where of course there's not one single glimmer of natural light, means no daily solar cycle. I found this extremely difficult to cope with, for instead of a normal 24-hour day, I was usually in a rolling one-in-three watch system – effectively four hours on, eight hours off, for anything up to 95 days; then every third day the watch would be split, so one watch was able to get 12 hours off when finishing at 8 p.m.

This obviously affects the natural performance of the brain, and I was having to eke out optimum performance at the same time as dealing with a new rolling 12-hour cycle. So, if I was going on watch every four hours and then having eight hours off, it basically rejigged the day from 24 hours into 12 hours. Jet lag then occurred, as it was akin to travelling across four time zones and then trying to adjust to that zone's living routines before taking off 12 hours later. I was in a constant state of lag, my body clock in meltdown; with mealtimes and sleep patterns changing constantly, I was waking up in the middle of the night, then going on watch in the control room in the dark. It was a complete nightmare. I'd spend the first hour trying to wake up, ingesting caffeine like it was going out of fashion.

All of this played havoc with most of my bodily functions. My bowels, for instance, would be shot to pieces; either blocked up, or I'd be holding on for dear life while doing an impression of the pipes in a pub when the barrels need changing. Fluctuations in sleeping patterns affect performance, there's no doubt it. Next time you read about a submarine that's run aground on the west coast of Scotland or been in a collision with a French nuclear sub,* it's probably been caused by a normally very switched-on, bright submariner in the mechanical or navigational team being knackered, and it's something they've either failed or forgotten to do because they've had a week of shit sleep. Let's just hope no such mistake ever happens in and around the workings of the nuclear reactor.

Dry skin and rashes were another side-effect, mostly as a result of the desiccated atmosphere in the boat and the recycled fresh air. Facially, I could be susceptible to dry skin

---

* It's always the French.

and scalp, and I could have given Philip E. Marlow's character in *The Singing Detective* a run for his money. Copious amounts of E45 cream usually did the trick. Another classic was the sebaceous cyst – the equivalent of having a marble-sized spot under the skin – usually on the neck area due to the constant rubbing of dirty naval-issue shirts. Popping one of those mothers was a joy to behold. If I was really lucky, the doctor would lance it; failing that, a fellow crewmate, provided he'd washed his hands first. It was still a long way from the Second World War, however, when scabies and crabs ran amok on naval vessels.

Cuts could take a while to heal because of the reduced oxygen content on board, which in the real world would have been higher and promoted quicker recovery. I remember slicing my finger while helping the chef – it bled for 48 hours before the wound closed. Everyone used to go down with a cold and a nasty cough after a week or so, as the crew got used to patrol conditions, in the same way as irritability usually came to the fore after three to four weeks. A combination of people missing loved ones, being cooped up with the same crew for three months and a lack of vitamin D made certain individuals more argumentative and prone to tit-for-tat bullshit. Unless you kept away from anyone you thought was a prize plum, you might find yourself having pointless arguments that you wouldn't have had at the start of patrol or indeed back on shore. And after a month the full effects of the interchangeable watch system would be kicking in with the reliability of a Swiss timepiece.

Most of my crewmates were totally cool throughout a patrol, but you always got the odd hothead whom it was best to avoid; most notably the sonar operator, who'd be constantly pissed before going to sea, getting so skulled he'd literally start eating his pint glass to prove how tough he was. I'd never seen anything like it – a complete nutter chewing on glass like a fairground geek, the rest of us edging slowly away from him before he decided to lay one of us out.

Except for sleeping quarters, the junior rates' dining hall on film night and the control room, from sunset onwards the boat was lit up with myriad lights like a fucking Christmas tree. This made you feel as if you were under interrogation lamps almost as soon as you crawled out of bed, exhausted from lack of sleep and faced not with granola, natural yoghurt and fruit, but toad-in-the-hole, mashed potatoes, apple crumble and custard. As lovely as that sounds, it takes some digesting after a five- or six-hour sleep.

The lighting needed to be as bright as possible in case of emergencies, so that every potential disaster could be quickly seen and – hopefully – isolated by damage-control teams, although in some emergencies the electrics had been short-circuited so we had no lighting at all and had to deal with it in pitch darkness. The constant, burning white light was yet another form of hell, ratcheting up the tension and making you feel as if you were on a brightly lit A&E ward. At mealtimes you'd have watches crossing over shifts, with those coming off watch all perky and jolly, relishing some downtime, while the sailors replacing them looked like complete shit – ghoulish, pasty and drawn, just out of bed and under the full glare of those cop-shop lights.

Compounding the discomfort of the lights was the smorgasbord of odours: body sweat, stale nicotine, farts, recycled oxygen. It took some getting used to. I could have periods of a few days or a couple of weeks when my body temperature would be all over the place, usually too hot, as I was awoken in the middle of the night, went to bed at 4 a.m., on watch till midnight, then back to bed at 4 p.m., day after day for three months. My body could never reach a state of equilibrium as I was either too tired, moody, pissed off and homicidal, or jokey, life and soul of the party, gregarious, cheeky and utterly reliable. All these states and emotions came and went without apparent rhyme or reason when we were locked down in the deeps, and a psychoanalyst could have had a field day with us if we'd taken one on patrol – 143 separate and indeed probably unique cases to interpret and treat.

I suffered from fatigue through my service, and most days it was a real struggle to get out of my bunk – even with burly Glaswegians right in my face, screaming at me to wake up. The way I tried to cope was to stay awake for as long as I could from 8 a.m. to midnight – whether that was on watch, studying, keeping fit, watching movies or drinking. If there was a spare couple of hours in the mid- or late-afternoon when I wasn't on watch, I'd try to grab a catnap and recharge the batteries. So long as I followed that schedule, things never got too bad, skin rashes and bowel issues aside, as I knew that occasionally I'd be getting racked out for a full eight-hour trip to the land of nod.

Every day, no matter our depth, the control room, where I kept my watches, was bathed in red lighting come sunset to synchronise the boat with above-water day- and night-times. Strange as it sounds, this was actually very soothing, and a pleasant change from the bright white lighting on the rest of the boat. The only issue came from rising from bed at night and going on watch; it then took longer to adjust as I went from the dark of my bunk, into the bright lights of the galley as dinner – my breakfast – was being served, then back to the dark, red, misty lighting of the control room. After a large meal I'd quickly become tired again, longing for my bunk. Bordering on the bizarre was when red lighting became black lighting, if a return to periscope depth occurred overnight. You wouldn't want a situation where the boat was near the surface at night, with white light reflecting through the periscope and potentially giving the submarine's position away. This usually happened when we were up for a routine satellite lock-on to check our latitude and longitude position.

Blackout curtains were rigged across the control room to ensure that the captain had the best view possible through the periscope, but this in turn made it impossible to see anything on a watch changeover. Changing watches in black lighting was usually a no-no, but on one occasion the captain deemed it OK, as we had to spend longer than usual at periscope depth. One able seaman relieving me in black lighting blindly stumbled, fell forward and brought the curtains down over the captain, completely covering his head and making him look like a murder suspect being led from a police van into court or something out of a Jacques Tati film. 'Get this fucking cretin off me!' he boomed. The poor lad was scrubbing decks for a week solid afterwards.

20

CUT OFF

Being cut off from the rest of the world was bleak, a submarine being widely recognised as one of the world's most demanding environments, both physically and psychologically. Working and surviving in cramped conditions with an absence of natural light, coupled with the monotony of watch and the intrinsic danger of everyday life on board given the emergencies that could lurk round the corner at any time – reactor scram, fire, flood, lack of oxygen supply, hydraulic failure and loss of propulsion – all added to the tension.

I loved the fact that although there were usually 143 crew on board, the captain, XO and navigator were the only ones who knew exactly where we were. I guess this was good for bonding, as no matter what our rank or length of service, we were all very literally in the same boat. What we did know, however, was that we had to be within range of the Soviet Union, anywhere within 1,950 nautical miles of Moscow, the main target area for our missiles. We'd been supplied with an updated Polaris system in 1982 that reduced the distance they flew by 500 nautical miles, and this had the knock-on effect of giving us much less water to hide in.

Optimism and a good sense of humour, washed down with a vat of healthy cynicism, were essential attributes for survival under the oceans. Maintaining a keen sense of team spirit was also vital – that, and the ability to get on with fellow sailors. A tight ship, where you could rely on all the crew to watch your back, was paramount. You couldn't be wondering whether the guy next to you was going to go walkabout if there was a fire or a flood or some other life-threatening emergency. On the flipside, you had to be completely on top of your own job – and have a good grasp of everyone else's too if the shit hit the fan. Yes, you could practise drills or damage-control exercises while at sea, but it was quite impossible to replicate the real thing. And nothing in initial training came near preparing you for the claustrophobia, for while there were various psychological tests conducted to see whether you might have a propensity to suffer in an enclosed space, you never really knew how you were going to react until it was time to dive. It might be that you were totally at ease, or it might be, like my friend Philip, that it gnawed so unbearably at your insides that there was no choice but to try to escape, no matter the consequences.

There were certain essential traits that every submariner required that were easy to spot, the main one being their positivity. When spending weeks under the ocean you needed to have an upbeat outlook on life and tell yourself: *Yes, the next three months are going to be a struggle, the conditions turgid, but I'm not going to let it affect me, I can't get depressed, I refuse to.* Admittedly, there were the minor bullying episodes on my first patrol, but I quickly forgot about those and let sleeping dogs lie. Harmony on the boat was paramount; you couldn't have a submarine where crewmates were constantly bickering with each other. Not only would it affect everyone else's morale – it could be potentially catastrophic in such a confined space if someone went postal and attacked another sailor.

I was lucky in so far as I was both fairly outgoing and a good listener. It was essential to remain both positive and calm, and restrain any feelings of negativity I might have had until I returned alone to the sanctity of my bunk. Healthy relationships with members of my own watch team were crucial, for they were the people I spent most of my time with. Off the boat a few of us would often hang out together, as well as having other friends on the sub that we drank and socialised with. I'm sure I got on people's nerves at times and vice versa. The key was to take a moment and try to relax if I found myself being wound up.

I tried to imagine that each compartment had its own unique personality and features, in the sense that different things happened there. The control room and most of 1 Deck were geared to work, so I kept my game face on at all times here; it was very much the captain's space, so no pissing about. It was also the home of the underwater telephone, which was usually left switched on during patrol, and the eerie sounds I heard emanating from it were awe inspiring and magical. The noises of whales, dolphins and porpoises communicating to one another in the deep made for a very welcome sideshow, and their mysterious, unfathomable conversation invariably kept me company during my watch. I often heard a carousel of cetacean sounds, and while they could be uplifting, the groans of the whales could be heart-breakingly sad, like lost souls of the deep. I wouldn't have missed it for the world.

Human sounds are generated through a mixture of air and vibration; vibration is then modified through the speech organs in the nasal cavities, which creates our voice – and my beautiful Black Country accent, in particular. A dolphin, porpoise or whale, with teeth rather than baleen plates, communicates by sending out short bursts of high-frequency clicks – very much like sonar – called echolocation, enabling them to map the environment around them and plot the direction in which they are travelling. The clicks that echo back are so detailed they can work out not only how far away the target is, but also its shape, size and movement. These mammals also communicate with whistling sounds, created by passing air through an area in the head called the phonic lips, which are similar to vocal chords in a human, creating a vibration that exits the head via the *melon*, which shapes and directs the sound. Baleen cetaceans like the blue, fin and humpback whales communicate by a series of grunts, groans, snorts and barks. But it's the humpback that has the longest and most musical song.

All of the above could be picked up on the underwater telephone. It was hard to understand why our massive weapon of war would be such a magnet for this range of marine fauna, but it was spectacular listening to them, each with their unique sounds, and after a bit of research we could start to work out which species was trying to get our attention. The creatures were probably a long way off, as sound can travel vast distances underwater, but I'd like to think they wanted to make friends with the new black beast beneath them. We'd have a massive increase in activity every time the shit tank was blown overboard, as various krill, crabs and plankton would make a beeline to snaffle up the crap.

I was lucky enough to keep watch only a few feet from the underwater telephone where all of this was relayed, and it was amazing to hear the short staccato bursts that emanated from dolphins, or indeed the baritone of the mighty sperm whales as they went about their business, oblivious to the goings-on in our steel tube. On many occasions I felt we were trespassing on their natural habitat, but I kept such sentiments to myself as I wanted to avoid the 'fucking hippie' tag that they would undoubtedly have provoked.

As I mentioned earlier, it was comforting for me to imagine that the various areas of the submarine had their own personalities, with different sensations, smells and functions. And if 1 Deck was all business – dominated by the control room, from where the boat was essentially run and where the fighting would be directed – 2 Deck was more of a space for living. I always felt more relaxed here as it was a place for pleasurable pursuits: eating, drinking, playing games or watching a movie. It was also somewhere I'd zone out and think about the future and where it would take me, what I'd be doing in 10, 20, 30 years' time. The smells were different down here too, for while 1 Deck was all fans and electrics, 2 Deck exuded a whiff of school canteen by day, and a bakery-cum-bar by night with a hint of beer and fags to accompany the dough.

3 Deck was the realm of the three Rs: rest, recuperation and reflection. Noise was frowned upon – at any given moment a third to a half of the crew would be tucked up in their bunks, asleep, reading, listening to music or having some private time, so it was important to be quiet. And it was always dark. When I wasn't sleeping or recharging my batteries for the next watch, I used to reflect on the day's events in the privacy of my bunk, working through any problems I had.

In terms of personality, the missile compartment was quite another matter. I always felt deeply uncomfortable in there, walking among the agents of death, the air cool like a mausoleum and eerily silent. Other than when I had to show up to learn the basics to get my dolphins, it was an area of the boat I was very happy never to have to visit much at all. The welcome was seldom great, either. I hardly ever spoke to the weapons engineers who kept watch behind roped-off areas armed with truncheons. They tended to be a quiet, insular bunch – no harm in that. Maybe they were preparing for any unauthorised personnel trying to jump the rope. If this did happen, the offender would be unceremoniously battered to the floor to within an inch of their lives. Compared with the rest of the boat it just wasn't somewhere I wanted to be – it gave me the creeps knowing what was lurking in the rows of tubes as I edged nervously through the compartment. Occasionally I'd caress them and stare down at the red numbers denoting the missile numbers, hoping their grim service would never be called upon, willing them to stay in their tubes, pristine and unused.

I'd sometimes thread my way up and down through the whole compartment, all three decks of it, taking in the enormity of what was held here. It was certainly strange to think that I could just stroll around among weapons that possessed more explosive power than all the bombs dropped in the Second World War. Surely no leader would be mad enough to invite the wrath of this jaw-dropping arsenal? Periodically the sense of doom and gloom would be lifted by the noise of the exercise bike, the rowing machine or the MEO up all hours playing delightful tunes on his Spanish guitar, the nails on his right hand grown long so he could expertly pluck the six strings. The missile compartment was always brilliantly lit, white-washed and stark as a laboratory. Not surprisingly it lacked the life and soul of the other compartments on board. I guess you don't bond with bombs.

Back aft was a completely different proposition, a sensory overload of heat, sweat, noise and smells. From AMS 2* right back to the motor room was like a different world, and it became progressively smaller the closer you got to the boat's propeller. The first thing that hit you was the heat generated by the reactor, coupled with the steam and turbo generators, and all the electrics required to maintain the life-support systems. It could get seriously hot back aft, regularly 30° or even 40°C. These were extreme conditions – only the galley could compete in terms of temperature – but they were necessary to keep the submarine up and running 24/7, for three months. Given that part of its function was maintaining our oxygen supply, removing CO_2 from the atmosphere and making water, I held this area of the submarine in awe. The working conditions were both oppressive and trying for engineers clad in boots and overalls, whose job involved climbing up and down ladders and squeezing themselves through cramped spaces. In the engine and motor room they had to crawl around on all fours just to operate valves and pumps – all of this to ensure us lot at the other end of the boat could live safely.

And in the middle of all this was the reactor compartment, which was maintained so it could supply steam to power the propulsion of the boat and its electrical supply.

* Auxiliary machinery space.

This was all conducted by the engineers in the manoeuvring room, an area that always fascinated me, the rows of dials like something from a 1960s NASA documentary. There were so many buttons and switches that you half-expected Gene Kranz, the legendary flight director of Apollo 11, to be sitting there directing operations. I could literally spend hours on a seat directly in front of the great luminous panel, staring at it intrigued but clueless as to the workings of all things nuclear.

It was always with great respect and a feeling of awe that I ventured into the bowels of the submarine, and I'd take regular trips back aft on all my patrols. The men who worked there were highly respected because of their talents and commitment to the cause, and, while this was true in general of the boat, it was more pronounced here, where a mixture of mutual respect and bonhomie reigned under Lt Cdr Hawthorn, the MEO and master of flamenco. Amid all the infernal heat, chaos and potential danger, the manoeuvring room remained the apex of chilled composure, with five or six men keeping the submarine functioning, and a further three keeping tabs in AMS 2, AMS 3 and the motor room.

The reactor panel operator (RPO) dealt solely with the functioning of the reactor. By regulating the rods to either increase or decrease the reactivity, he was responsible for how much power it generated. In some cases, such as training simulations, kit or machinery failure, or power overload, he would have to scram the reactor and shut it down. The electrical panel operator (EPO) made sure all the electrical systems coming out of the reactivity of the reactor were working correctly, while also balancing the electrical supplies required by the whole submarine. The throttle control panel operator (TCPO) was the least qualified person of the team. Under orders from the OOW in the control room, he was responsible for moving the throttles to operate the main engines and ensure the correct amount of steam made its way to them. In charge was the nuclear chief of the watch (NCOW) – a seasoned chief petty officer, professionally qualified in nuclear watch-keeping, who could effortlessly take over any of the above roles. He in turn reported to the engineering officer of the watch, who was also a trained nuclear watch-keeper, highly qualified in all aspects of nuclear power management on subs and well versed in dealing with the sorts of emergencies that may or may not occur come the Day of Reckoning.

In the five years I spent in the Submarine Service, I seldom walked more than a few yards in a straight line on a sub or with my head at its natural height. For when I wasn't making way for fellow crewmates in corridors, I'd be ducking through bulkheads, clambering up and down ladders, banging my head on protruding pipes or jutting-out valves. It was a constant headache – literally – just to traverse the boat in this cramped undersea world.

No running, either. That was frowned upon, and even in an emergency drill the most you could get away with was walking quickly. I once saw a guy with a pencil in his mouth tearing down 2 Deck on his way to the control room. Another chap who'd just got out of bed from the senior rates' mess stepped in his path. They collided, and the pencil was shoved right back into the man's mouth – he was lucky he didn't choke to death. When he'd recovered from his coughing fit he suffered an almighty rollocking from the coxswain for his trouble. I never run anywhere now, apart from around Victoria Park in Hackney.

It was a world within a world, where I was not only isolated from the rest of humanity but at times cut off from others members of the crew too. Working on a shift pattern during the three months of patrol, you might not see one of your good mates for days at a time. I might catch a glimpse of him at a mealtime, when we'd exchange a laugh, an insult or a bit of harmless gossip, and then if we were on a different watch pattern I might not see him again for a few days. It was like your friends would completely disappear, then suddenly pop up again out of the blue at breakfast, where we'd finish our stories over a tin of grapefruit seggies and some kidneys on toast.

Since I was quite a social person, this intermittent human contact would occasionally cause me considerable angst. Loneliness was quite difficult to deal with, and while I might have projected a hard, unflappable exterior, inside I was wondering whether putting myself through the emotional wringer was worth it. It just didn't stack up. Machismo drove me to drink and work out. Being a submariner in the Cold War was no place for the emotionally delicate, and if

I'd mentioned my concerns to the wrong person they would have had me off that boat in a flash. Back in the 1980s the military was fairly indifferent to sailors with any sorts of emotional issue, and it certainly wasn't the kind of environment in which I could sit down and offload my worries to a superior rank without running the risk of getting sent back sharpish to general service. But it did help to talk to one of my mess mates about them, as it mostly turned out they were feeling pretty much the same. Sharing problems made them easier to cope with, and we worked together to stave off our sense of isolation. Lots of people in many walks of life suffer from perceived feelings of abandonment, anguish and isolation, but experiencing such distress while deep under the world's oceans could have been catastrophic. Staying busy was key to keeping all this at bay.

As well as studying in my spare time, reading books and listening to my Walkman played a very important role in keeping me sane, as well as opening up my mind to other worlds, both real and fictional. Reading became a bit of an obsession, both to escape any unwanted thoughts that might otherwise have crept into my head and as a release from the stresses produced by the confinement of submarine life. I couldn't just finish my watch and immediately go to bed – time was more precious to me than that. Nor could I simply switch off mentally. I had to gently come down. Reading was my way of helping me retain an inner peace, as well as keeping me in touch with the world beyond the deep, far, far away.

I enjoyed reading books about the sea. Herman Melville's classic tale *Moby Dick* was an obvious one, at once alluring and charming, its language full of a simple beauty, and stuffed to the gunwales with flashes of great humour. A compelling study of obsessive passion, it illustrates just how far an individual can be driven at the cost of everything else; in Ahab's case, his crew, his ship, and ultimately his own life. I gave my copy to the captain when I finished it. Fortunately he loved it, and didn't think I was casting aspersions on him.

Hemingway was another author I loved. I'd read him at school and was eager to get reacquainted. *The Old Man and the Sea* is a special book, telling of the monumental struggle between Santiago, an ageing fisherman who hasn't caught a thing for 84 days, and the magnificent marlin he finally hooks off the coast of Cuba. For three days it's man versus beast until he finally lands and kills it, then sets off on the long sail back to shore. During this journey the marlin, strapped to the side of his skiff, is picked at by sharks, and by the time he arrives home there's only the skeleton left. Santiago comes full circle from zero to hero, heralded on his return as a hero by the other local fisherman who have measured the great fish and reckon it to be over five metres long. Hemingway's point is that victory is not a prerequisite for honour, but seeing a task through to its very end with pride and determination is. A bit like a 90-day submarine patrol.

Another book I read to keep me grounded was Edward Young's *One of Our Submarines*. I used to regularly dip in and out of it while at sea, and it was a great help in putting patrol life and any difficulties I might have into some sort of perspective. The book was a classic account of his time in submarines during the Second World War, and what made it all the more remarkable was that despite being a member of the Royal Navy Reserve, he rose up the ranks to command a boat. It's also stayed with me, as Young worked in the publishing industry – as I do now – before the war, where he designed books for Penguin and invented the famous logo for the new paperback imprint founded by Allen Lane, following an afternoon spent at London Zoo. He also came up with the idea of the famous colour-coded jackets: orange for novels, green for crime, and pale blue for the Pelican series of accessible books on academic subjects.

In 1943 Young was the first person from the Royal Navy Reserve to skipper a submarine. The book looks back at his submarine career on the old U- and S-class boats, which were horrible, cramped and smelly diesel subs, weighing from 740 to 975 tonnes, absolutely tiny when compared with the 8,500-tonne deterrent that I was on. Young writes with modesty and good humour about the lack of decent food, torturous conditions and absence of washing facilities. It's very much like reading *Das Boot* from a British perspective.

Writing matter-of-factly about his first submarine, HMS *Umpire*, being involved in a collision with an armed trawler in the North Sea, I could only admire his – and his fellow crewmates' – courage while their boat sank, as I knew, and was told many times, how flooding on a submarine can prove fatal. And so it proved on 19 July 1941. After hitting the trawler on the surface, *Umpire* rapidly sank to the bottom of the North Sea in 80 feet of water. Young found himself in command, as the captain had been on the bridge at the time the sinking began. Young attempted to surface the submarine, but the water was flooding in too rapidly. He found himself with three other crew in the conning tower, surrounded by a fast-rising torrent of sea water that would drown them in minutes.

He made the decision to shut the lower lid of the conning tower, then force open the upper lid and swim up to the surface. Somehow they prised open the hatch – it reminded me of the SETT training in HMS *Dolphin* at the start of my career, but this was the real thing, far more pressing, and literally a matter of life and death. One man was never seen again, another drowned on reaching the surface, but Young survived with a fellow able seaman, plus seven crew who had escaped out of the engine room hatch. In total 22 submariners died that day. Young went on to pass the Perisher course and take command of HMS *Storm*, which operated first in Norway and then moved to the Far East, mainly in and around the coasts of Sri Lanka (known as Ceylon at the time of the war) as part of the 4th Submarine Flotilla engaged in hunting down the Japanese Navy and its merchant fleet.

It's a classic tale of life aboard a submarine under extreme duress, and if I was ever feeling down or depressed I used to pick it up, if just to read what Young and his crew had to deal with and how grim life must have been. It soon put my own troubles into perspective.

Like everyone else in the boat – and indeed in the entire Submarine Service at that time – I read Tom Clancy's intelligent and brilliantly written military thriller *The Hunt for Red October*. It was his first-ever book, published just a year before I joined the Navy, and the buzz around it in the UK was just starting when I began my submarine career. The plot centres around Ramius, a Soviet submarine captain who has become disenchanted with the communist state, blaming it for the death of his wife of many years, and he hatches a plan to defect with his submarine to the United States. The book caused quite a stir at the time among the crew and throughout the submarine community as a whole, as it implied that the Soviets were an unhappy bunch who were uncommitted to their cause. This couldn't have been further from the truth – in our experience they seemed anything but: relentless and determined as they hunted down Allied submarines across the oceans.

The book also drew attention to the building of the new Soviet Typhoon-class submarines, which represented a massive step forward in terms of the country's military might. The size alone of these boats beggared belief, weighing 48,000 tonnes, dived, dwarfing *Resolution*'s 8,500 tonnes, while their beam was 74 feet wide, compared with *Resolution*'s 33 feet. They were powered by not one but two nuclear reactors for the two propellers needed to drive these massive beasts forward. They had a games room with arcade games in it, a gym fitted with wall bars, weights, rowing machines and punch bags, and a sauna and large bath-cum-mini-swimming-pool, like one of those changing-room baths that permed footballers in the 1970s would dive into after a cup win. It all sounds quite pleasant, making submarines of this class much more like floating hotels than messengers of Armageddon.

The Typhoons' nuclear payload was 20 R-39 missiles with a range of 5,200 miles. Each missile had ten warheads with 100 to 200 kilotonnes of explosive power apiece. So, theoretically, they could stay in their base at Severodvinsk on the banks of the Northern Dvina River near Archangel, and launch their missiles, easily striking and utterly wiping out Washington DC, along with the majority of big cities in the US, all while still alongside. Population centres in the countries of Western Europe – Britain, France, Germany, the Netherlands and Belgium – could also be nonchalantly taken out while they were at it. The boat was further stocked with torpedoes and cruise missiles. This single piece of Soviet engineering was the biggest threat to peace in the final five years of the Cold War. Happily, during my time at sea, we never knowingly came across one, but knowing they were out there certainly concentrated the mind.

21

RACKED OUT

The only place – indeed the only space – I could truly call my own was my bunk, or 'rack' as it was more commonly known on board, in 9 Berth, named for its nine bunks, on 3 Deck. Here I could escape from the rest of the crew and actually find time to contemplate the day's events, read a book, listen to music and have some private time. But first and foremost I came here to sleep. I was eternally shattered from the never-ending watch-keeping cycle, and needed my eight hours off in between watches – that, or I'd be catnapping in the afternoon to prepare for a long night ahead in the control room.

It was cramped all right, me and the rest of the tactical systems team crammed into 9 Berth. The size of a chunky walk-in wardrobe, I likened it to being half the size but roughly the same shape as the box you serve into in a game of tennis. It measured three paces forward by either side, and that was just the space in which we could walk or indeed fall around in when it was pitch dark (all the time), trying to get pants, socks, trousers, shirt and sandals on ready to go on watch.

Entering 9 Berth, I'd first be hit by the overarching hum of human flesh in need of a 30-minute soak in a large, soapy bath, quickly followed by the secondary whiff of spunked-in socks, shirts and trousers hanging on pegs, mixed with a hint of bad breath, sweaty balls and arse. A rare cocktail indeed. Three bunks faced me on entry, with three to the port side and three on the starboard. At the bottom of the bunks there were sets of tiny drawers, one for each member of the crew. I tended to stow my boots and overalls in the drawer to keep them separated.

Within the berth there was an overwhelming sense of the walls closing in, and at any given time there might be a maximum of six people sleeping in this tiny space, with the other three out on watch. My bunk was situated dead ahead of me as I walked into the space, about 6 feet off the ground. When I first joined it was a baptism of fire even getting into the bloody thing. The bunk itself was around 6 feet long by 3 feet wide, and the headspace between the mattress and the top of the bunk couldn't itself have been much more than 3 feet. A squash and a squeeze, to put it mildly.

Inside the bunk was a sleeping bag, pillow, a light for reading and then a 'punkah louvre' – think of the outlet you sit under in an aircraft that supposedly pumps out fresh air while you fly – that blew recycled fresh air out into the bunk to try to stop its resident from overheating. I could barely turn over to sleep on either side without banging my shoulder or arm or head on some part of the Formica panelling above. I'm 5 foot 11 inches and was at that point very slim, so if I had trouble manoeuvring myself in here, spare a thought for my taller and larger crewmates, curled up like massive oversized adults trying to sleep in a child's bed – very *Gulliver's Travels*. They constantly had to change position to get comfy in the hope of getting some kip – it must have been a nightmare. The closest you'd get in the real world would be one of those pod hotels in Tokyo, but while they're similar in length and width, they're much more generous with head space, so they don't feel too claustrophobic. There was nothing funny about Lilliputian bunks and big, bleary-eyed seamen becoming irascible with their constant lack of sleep. A reduction in general alertness and brain function equalled a higher likelihood of serious fuck-ups while on watch.

It was like getting racked out in a coffin – you were crammed in, light out, curtain pulled closed … and buried alive. Well, that's what it felt like the first night I dived on work-up before my first patrol. I remember thinking there was no way I was going to hack this for the duration; time to rethink the career choice. But I soon grew to love it here in this tiny, dank and dark space, as I could switch off from the Groundhog Day monotony of the patrol cycle and drift off into the land of nod.

My bunk in 9 Berth was situated very close to AMS 1* on 3 Deck, home to bits of machinery like the bilge pump and hydraulic plants, whose soporific humming wove a hypnotic

* Auxiliary machinery space.

spell over me, making it easy to get off to sleep at will. This was coupled with the fact that I was usually totally shattered – or at least slightly the worse for wear – when I finally hauled myself up for some shut-eye. As I was on the top bunk I'd have to reach up and grab the very small hand grip, then hoist my legs up, point them into the bunk and jack-knife in, followed by my head and shoulders. Finally, it would be curtain pulled back and then – for the first time in hours – glorious privacy. Lots of the crew slept in T-shirts and pants. Fuck that. The clothes I wore were smelly enough without sleeping in them as well. Nope, it was the bollocky buff for me, naturally with pants at the ready if I had to get up smartish or woke up with a hard-on. My sleeping bag had to last the whole patrol – it wouldn't be washed for the duration – and 90 days sleeping in the same bag was a stretch. I tried to air mine as best I could between watches, unzipping it and leaving it open, with the air vent pointing downwards to give it some biff.

If the boat changed depth, ascending to or back down from periscope depth, it always used to wake me, but the slow, beguiling inclines of the boat as we reached for the skies or the depths of the ocean below were incredibly comforting while I drifted in and out of consciousness. The sub is in many ways like an aeroplane in terms of the end-to-end and sideways movement … one wing up, one wing down, while on a boat the foreplanes and afterplanes do the same job, although mostly without the turbulence. A submarine also has three-dimensional movement:

forwards, backwards and lateral, plus the ability to travel in a vertical plane, up towards the surface and down to its test depth.

Many captains used the phrase 'She flies very well' when commenting on *Resolution*'s manoeuvrability, and it was a joy just to lie back and enjoy the ride. The changes of depth and course were so smooth we could have been travelling business class – without the views, of course.

Everyone had to be as quiet as possible down in the bunk spaces, and you'd quickly become the resident arsehole if you were found to be making a din. Silence often proved difficult to maintain with the buzz of coming off watch or following a few jars, especially as some of the crew were racked out in the passageway; imagine the hustle and bustle of hairy-arsed submariners careering past and flopping into their bunks. Being racked out downwind of the toilets could have serious disadvantages, particularly if we were in sonar silent state, when flushing was not allowed.

Coffin dreams were not something we talked about in great detail – these nightmares made sailors shout or lash out in fear that they were being buried alive or slowly suffocated by a gradually reducing space, the walls literally coming in from each side. I used to have dreams that the roof of my bunk was closing in on me, and on a few occasions I fell out of the top bunk to get away, waking up as I hit the deck hard, which startled both me and my crewmates. Some people used to scream and shout so much in their sleep that you had to wake them up.

I remember having a dream in which I saw my own funeral take place, only to discover that I was still alive in a glass-lined transparent coffin, thrashing around like a madman, my face covered in white greasepaint like a clown. No one could see I was alive but me, looking down on myself on top of the hearse. I woke up screaming and dripping with sweat, so much so that I thought I'd shat myself. This dream has stayed with me to this day. I put it down to the general stress of the living environment, my body clock being all over the place and eating at irregular times; when combined, these could certainly lead to some strange goings-on in the bunks at night.

There was one guy who occasionally sleepwalked, which was a bit unnerving as I was never quite sure what he might do. He did it one night when we were away on a training course in Plymouth, and went and sat on the window-sill, opening and closing the curtains. I kept an eye on him from my bed in case he opened one of the windows, as we were a few floors up. He didn't, but proceeded instead to get up, walk to the middle of the room, piss on the floor and get back into bed. Had he sleepwalked on board he'd have been intercepted pretty quickly as there was always someone milling around, and hopefully they'd have caught him before he fell down a ladder or appeared at the skipper's cabin wanting to relieve himself.

Away for three months at a time, surrounded by stinking sailors … so what else went on in my bunk? It doesn't require a great deal of imagination, but everyone needs some 'private time' to themselves. It was universally known that masturbation was rife on board, which was only natural, although I do remember a shipmate saying he'd gone one whole 70-day patrol without indulging. His daily updates after about week two started to get on everyone's wick, and he quickly became the patrol bore. No one believed him, but he was adamant; his first cum face post-patrol must have been a picture. On the flip side, you could tell who overindulged; thanks to their ferocious bashing the bishop just an hour before, they'd be walking bandy-legged along the passageways on their way to keep watch, looking just like John Wayne.

Some people made more noise than others, and one guy in our berth used to leave his light on when he was in full swing; it looked like a puppet show from the other side of the curtain. There'd also be the tell-tale sign of curtains twitching and the right elbow hoving in and out of view. At this point, if I'd just arrived in 9 Berth, I usually walked around and returned in five minutes, giving them time to finish up. Each submariner would have their own 'wanker-chief', 'wank hanky' or plain 'jizz rag', an essential bit of kit that one used to clean up, varying in material from a bit of cotton to civvy socks or the girlfriend's underwear. This was usually stowed under the mattress or the pillow, something I didn't object to as I was on the top bunk. I was a lot more respectful to crewmates with the use of toilet roll which, unlike the wank hanky, was easily flushable. Any residue would have the habit of trickling down from above, not great for someone on a lower bunk; their sleeping bag could assume the look of a plasterer's radio come week five. Onanism aside, I was lucky I was a deep sleeper – someone could have been playing the drums next to my head and I wouldn't have woken up. I guess I averaged around six hours sleep per day, which wasn't too bad under the circumstances.

Waking time in the bunk was mostly spent either reading or, that other great saviour, listening to music. It was always slightly annoying trying to read in there as the space was so confined, but listening to music was perfect. With the Walkman next to my head and headphones on, I'd be out like a light in no time. My music collection was fairly substantial for a patrol. I used to take around 50 cassette tapes with me, crammed into my passageway locker along with my washing kit and changes of clothes. Music was everything to me, and I'd loved it ever since my father bought me an old Glen Campbell live album when I was about ten.

Growing up in and around the Midlands in the late 1970s and early 80s, I soon became aware that music stood for so much more than just the sounds – it was also culture, the clothes, the way you identified yourself. As a kid I loved The Jam and was always influenced not just by their music but also by what the band wore, in particular Paul Weller. I would go into Beatties department store in the Mander Centre in Wolverhampton to get the two-tone Jam shoes and the boating blazer. I never liked the Mod haircut, though, being far too self-conscious to dare wear it on the streets of the West Midlands. Someone would have taken offence and mouthed off, so I plumped for the ska suede-head. I also loved the early look of Dexys Midnight Runners' *On the Waterfront*-style vibe, with pea coat, woolly hat or box jacket and duffel bag, plus I'd never heard anyone sing like Kevin Rowland; he was of Anglo-Irish descent and spent much of his childhood in Wolverhampton, just the same as me. With his rich and incredibly powerful voice that could cover the octaves, he was a sort of male version of Kate Bush, whom I also adored.

The West Midlands had been home to reggae, two-tone and ska, so I'd grown up listening to bands such as Ranking Roger, Steel Pulse, UB40, The Specials and The Beat. My father loved his classical music, which I'd initially hated, but since my school years I'd grown increasingly to appreciate it, and under the oceans it became a real godsend: Elgar, Mendelssohn, Chopin, Vaughan Williams or Bruch could all reduce me to a blubbering wreck in my bunk.

I listened and re-listened to the albums I took on patrol, and would play them over and again until the Walkman mangled the tape. I can still recall every single word of Tom Waits's *Closing Time* and Kate Bush's *Hounds of Love*, and even now, when I hear them many years on, they immediately transport me back into that tiny cramped space of my bunk.

22

FOOD, GLORIOUS FOOD

The most important aspect of a submariner's stint at sea is the standard and quality of the food he eats, and the chefs have it in their power to influence morale like no other department in the boat. I found it was always prudent to keep on the right side of the chefs; for any hungry sailor, they were as important as the captain. Meals were the one break in the chain that stopped us feeling permanently at sea. A nuclear submarine then – as now – is essentially a living being. It maintains its own life-support systems for oxygen, clean air, getting rid of CO_2 and making its own water, and generates power through the use of a reactor that could run almost for ever, give or take. The only thing preventing it from being at sea indefinitely is the crew's need for food, or 'scran', as it was known

The taste and smell of good food meant everything to us, each meal being one of the high points of the day, and when you found yourselves as cut off from the rest of the world as we were, the importance of food was magnified many times over. Three times a day the junior and senior rates' mess and the wardroom came alive, abuzz with the joy of this great ritual of communal living. And while the wardroom enjoyed the luxury of silver service, served to them by the stewards, we all ate the same food and drank the same alcohol. Mealtimes were crucial in bonding all those who worked on the boat, instilling a sense of morale, purpose and togetherness that was essential in creating an atmosphere where the submarine could operate to its full potential.

The supply officer and the PO chef chose all the food from a core list of produce that was almost identical each patrol: meat, fish, vegetables, fresh fruit and salad for the first fortnight of patrol before the food went off, then various dried foodstuffs, tinned or frozen food and fruit, flour, UHT milk cartons, confectionary, eggs, flour and so on for the much longer period thereafter. Plus, not least, the booze; tens of thousands of cans of beer and lager, together with bottles of wine and beer kegs all had to be loaded on board. Then there would be a luxury list – including fillet steak or racks of lamb, with some mighty fine French or Italian red wines – for the three formal mess dinners and the special slap-up meal that took place once on every patrol.

What was absolutely essential was that the food numbers were correct. Woe betide any cock-ups with the numbers. Running out of food once led to the crew spending the last couple of weeks of patrol moaning every mealtime, and on one patrol we had to stay out an extra three weeks because HMS *Revenge* had some mechanical problem, *again*. By the last week we were down to a single meal per day, and there were a lot of thin, pasty-faced and pissed-off-looking submariners on the casing as we headed back up the gangplank.

The scran and booze all had to be loaded up on board the boat over a period of usually two to three days when we were alongside. Lorries would turn up in the order that the supplies needed to be loaded onto the boat. Before my days as quartermaster I was involved in storing the ship for sea, like most people who lived and worked forward of the missile compartment. It was a major challenge, for while submarines are among the most technically advanced bits of machinery in the world, not a single one of them has any major access points into which big cranes can swing a load containing the stores that the boat relies on. As a result there was nothing mechanical about the process – it was just good old hard manual labour and sheer brute force that got everything on board, and it all had to pass through the main access hatch, whose diameter was around 30 inches.

When the storing was complete, the submarine would be holding food in the dry-storage room, fridge space, the freezers and indeed any other spare nook and cranny that could be found – there was enough food to feed a family of four for up to five years. By the time of morning departure for a patrol, supplies might include 1,600 kilos of beef, 2,300 kilos of potatoes, 10,000 eggs, 1,000 chickens, 2 miles of sausages, 4,900 pints of milk, 1 tonne of beans, 60,000 tea bags and around 5,000 toilet rolls – possibly the most essential bit of kit and really not something to even consider getting your calculations wrong about.

Before my first patrol I was in the unenviable position of being first on the ladder through the main access hatch, so I enjoyed the full force and weight of all the heavy boxes being passed down to me. I would then have to somehow twist and counterbalance my weight under the load and pass the boxes down, while also trying not to fall on the next guy in line in the hatch. It was extremely awkward space-wise, so much so that my forearms and biceps would be black and blue by the end of the day, and copping any number of big clunks to the head would be commonplace.

Occasionally, things would get out of hand, with the ship's company falling out because somebody hadn't passed a box down properly. It sounds childish, but it was just the tension gathering with an impending long spell at sea looming heavily over us. Once sorted out, it was everyone back to it, with great kegs of beer being stuffed into spare space in the walls of the senior rates' mess or used as stools, toilet rolls wedged in at the end of bunks, food fitted within little compartments under the seats in the senior rates' mess and the wardroom, while the provisions store was full to the gills with food that didn't need to be frozen or chilled. False decks were installed by the chefs in the store room, where non-perishable tins would be stacked on top of each other to eke out every little bit of valuable extra space.

The physical impact that loading had on the crew was massive. After three days solid, perched on a ladder humping stores from dusk till dawn, I was always completely wasted. The same was going on back aft, with the engineers stocking up on screws, valve replacements and spare parts, because if any major works were needed when something went wrong on the submarine, things could get out of hand and become fatal pretty quickly without adequate tools or spare equipment to fix the problem. To keep the naval class structure well and truly in place, storing ship was the job of the junior rates. I do remember some of the warfare branch NCOs helping, and the PO chef himself would occasionally muck in, but mainly it was the junior rates doing all the heavy lifting.

The chefs and the supply officer would be down below, heading up the packing in the various areas, notably the dry store room, fridge and refrigerator space. It was essential these were packed by them, because they had to access the food in the correct order it would be used on patrol.

Food was paramount in helping establish the routine of the submarine, in particular the weekly calendar when certain days became synonymous with various meals – I could invariably tell which day of the week it was just by the smells wafting from the galley. Wednesday was curry night, for example, Friday fish night, Saturday steak night and Sunday roast dinner followed by pizza. Tuesday evenings we might have a theme, say Italian night, so it would be spaghetti bolognese, or chilli con carne on Mexican night (minus the sombreros).

The role of chef could be a lonely one; whereas most other departments go on and off watch en masse, as well as eating and sharing entertainment time together, the chefs – especially at night – tended to keep solo shifts. I always used to make a point of going down for a chat and a cuppa in the early hours as the chef was prepping breakfast or making fresh bread. Time could drag for him otherwise. I know we all like a bit of solitary time, but not having anyone around for hours at a time can quite quickly lead to depression.

The galley itself was on 2 Deck, at the bottom of the ladder from 1 Deck, and was around the size of a kitchen you'd find in a studio flat. Every day, 429 separate meals were cooked here, and on a 70-day patrol around 30,030 individual meals would be prepared, plus the three mess dinners, which took place towards the end of the trip. Incredible. The conditions in the galley were some of the worst on the boat in terms of pure heat; it could get seriously oppressive in there, up to 40°C. Snacks were also served most days, in the morning around ten, and then at four in the afternoon, when biscuits, cakes or caramel slices were made available.

I was at a chef's-table dinner at Claridge's in my present job, and found myself in the bowels of the hotel outside their kitchen, and it reminded me of the basics of a submarine galley in terms of its look and feel – stainless steel all the way, ovens and ranges, hot plates, potato peeler, meat slicers and, of course, a deep-fat fryer for fish and chips. Preparation areas were few and far between on board, so the chefs made do with what space they could, everything compacted to the inch.

Microwaves were not allowed as they were high-powered electrical items and could cause an emergency somewhere else if fuses were tripped. If the boat had to rapidly change depth, or went to and from periscope depth, then what were known as 'lock-in bars' in the galley could be attached to the stoves to stop pots of food flying around. These also worked well if we were caught on the surface in foul weather with the boat rolling around. And although many of the crew wouldn't have eaten anything in such circumstances, you can bet your life a chef would be in situ in the galley, cooking up a storm regardless of the weather up top.

It was just as important in the galley, as anywhere else in the boat, to be aware of making too much noise to avoid detection. In many ways the galley was just another bit of kit that had to be well looked after and treated delicately; food preparation needed to be chilled and cool, with no wild swings of the steak tenderiser or the meat slicers – any loud noise could have had an effect on the acoustic footprint given off by the submarine.

I was once lucky enough to meet the late, great American chef Anthony Bourdain, who likened his kitchens to a submarine galley: lifeless air, cramped and hot, with the staff holding outsiders in contempt. He told me he employed a couple of ex-submariner chefs as they could put up with any conditions and still deliver service on time and with a smile. Fair dos.

Unlike conventional kitchens, the galley had to be aware of the ship's atmospheric composition before preparing and cooking certain foods. If, for example, the CO_2 levels on board were too high, the full English breakfast that everyone was waiting for, or fish night on a Friday, would have to be put on hold as CO_2 levels rise rapidly when frying – limiting CO_2 production always trumped bacon and sausage or fish and chips. The other main difference to a professional kitchen was the use of water. Water was not in such abundant supply in a submarine and was used principally for maintaining life-support and engineering services back aft – what little was left was used for cooking, showers, shaving and teeth-brushing. The galley therefore had a limited amount of water to prepare and wash food, as well as to clean all the pots, pans and plates. Washing up crockery and cutlery after mealtimes was done in something that quickly resembled soup; this was tolerable if you were first to finish and you could use water that looked vaguely fresh, but if you were a late finisher, your plate usually came out dirtier than when you'd finished eating.

Submariners are a pretty lazy bunch in terms of food experimentation; we like things traditional and simple, so chefs would follow their military instruction manuals to the letter. That said, Elizabeth David and *Larousse Gastronomique* usually made it onto patrol, just in case any culinary extravagances were to be attempted (usually on mess dinner nights).

Breakfast consisted of an artery-hardening fry-up, with all the trimmings: fried bread, tins of beans, tins of tomatoes, black pudding and eggs made to order, as well as fresh bread baked overnight. Kidneys on fried bread ('shit on a raft', as it was known) was another option, but not for the faint-hearted; having the constitution of an ox was a prerequisite, otherwise an uncomfortable morning lay ahead playing tag-team with Trap 2 in the toilet. The meal was accompanied by fresh fruit and orange juice for the first couple of weeks; it was essential to build up vitamin C levels before the fresh fruit ran out, after which we resorted to tins of grapefruit, fruit cocktail or mandarin segments.

Lunch would be a choice from two of the following options: filled baked potatoes; corned beef hash; Welsh rarebit with a slice of ham, topped off with a fried egg, known as 'cheesy hammy eggy' – a naval staple (I always had mine with Worcester sauce); pasta provençal; 'Nellie's wellies' – spam fritters that looked like an elephant's foot-print; 'snorker pie' – sausage mince with beans in a pie, 'snorker' being a naval term for sausage; casserole – usually sausages; toad-in-the-hole; spaghetti in tomato sauce; chicken satay; pies – mince beef or chicken; sweet chilli chicken with rice; filled baguettes; pasta bake of the day; macaroni pudding; and salad – just the basics: lettuce, peppers, cucumbers and tomatoes, no danger of an avocado – for the first two weeks of patrol until it all went off.

The high point of every day was dinner, a veritable feast of gout-inducing pleasure to be savoured and enjoyed, especially if I was coming off watch with a 12-hour break before my next one. A few jokes with the boys and some back and forth with the chefs, it would be the equivalent of going out for dinner at a restaurant, followed by a few beers; the only thing missing being the company of women, though the leading weapons engineer could suffice after a few drinks. The meal was a varied and brilliant selection under the circumstances, and like lunch it would be a mixture of fresh and frozen food, until all the fresh ran out – then it would be just tinned and frozen mixed together.

Dinner was where the day's most satisfying conversations took place, as it brought the crew together in a shared bonding experience during which the latest developments on patrol could be discussed: last night's film, the latest round of football results we'd picked up off the World Service or 'Isn't that newbie officer a bell-end?' It was communal living like no other in the British military. Even though the conditions were challenging, being together as one under the world's oceans felt special, and I really didn't care if we were down to powdered egg or UHT milk. They were the best of times.

Apart from our extended and much-regretted excursion on one patrol, I never said or heard a bad word about the food. Everybody knew the chefs did their best under very difficult working conditions, and to make any kind of snide comment was just fucking rude, a major no-no. I heard tales from other submariners, moaning about the food that they got on their boats. That was sacrilege. I always loved the food, although I had to work out a lot, otherwise I could easily finish patrol having put on 20 pounds. You'll see why in a moment.

Dinner would take the form of the following, each and every week, in no particular order: minted lamb, chicken pie or lamb stew, with roast potatoes, mashed potatoes, roast carrots and broccoli; battered cod with chips, mushy pea and curry sauce; chicken curry, beef Madras or chicken korma with naan bread, poppadoms and saffron rice; chilli con carne with sour cream and grated cheese; sirloin steak; chicken Kiev. Sunday was roast, with either gammon, beef or lamb, roast potatoes, sprouts, carrots and gravy, and the choice on pizza night was ham and mushroom or pineapple and pepperoni.

If all of that hasn't got you racing out in search of the nearest defibrillator, the following list of desserts just might: jam roly poly; lemon meringue pie; fresh fruit salad (or tinned with evaporated milk, depending on how far into patrol we were); rice pudding with sultanas and jam sauce; apple or mixed fruit crumble and custard; key lime pie; jam and coconut sponge and custard; blancmange; Angel Delight ('ballerina shit', as it was known); and various cakes and gateaux.

It was a constant battle to resist gorging myself over the duration of the entire trip, although a few did succumb and ended up looking like heart attacks waiting to happen. Indeed, there are a number of people I've known, from captain down to able seaman, who've worked on nuclear submarines and have experienced cardiac problems at a fairly young age. It might have been the extreme working conditions – or maybe just one too many jam roly polys.

I'm sure much has changed in the modern era, but a submarine used to be no place for vegetarians. I decided to go veggie on one patrol, mainly down to my love of The Smiths, and Morrissey in particular. My parents had also recently become vegetarians, more for health reasons than any fondness for Manchester's favourite sons, although my mum has always loved 'Heaven Knows I'm Miserable Now'.

It wasn't a particularly well-planned move, as I'd informed neither the supply officer nor the PO chef of my newfound vegetarianism before they'd stored for sea. So I spent most days having fruit seggies for breakfast and spaghetti in tomato sauce for lunch. The killer came at dinner, where meat dominated, and I had to make do with a desultory plate of cauliflower cheese. I lasted about two weeks and, having soon shed half a stone from my already slim frame, I resembled a golf club. I was also particularly irritable and generally annoying, digging at crewmates at every opportunity, effing and blinding – I'd turned into the boat's grouch. Luckily for me, a mate shoved a steak and kidney pie in front of me and basically stood there until I ate it. I felt it oozing through my body, and slowly I regained my strength. Doubtless it's different now, but going veggie on deterrent patrol in the Cold War was probably not the wisest of choices.

I loved the smell of food on board, as it brought back memories of being back on land. Food was one of two things – along with the weekly familygrams – that kept the crew from going batshit. As most of the time I was breathing in stale, recycled air mixed with body odour, cigarette smoke, farts and various electrical and engineering smells, my sense of smell had become desensitised. What kicked it back into shape were those heavenly aromas emanating from the galley, a premonition of what was to follow …

The chefs would also help out on ship control, assisting with steering the boat either at dived depth or when returning to periscope depth for a BRN pass to establish our position. They were hard-working but played equally hard, much to the rest of the crew's enjoyment – boy, did they like a drink, smoke and a good laugh.

Towards the latter stages of patrol, the submarine held mess dinners for the wardroom, senior and junior rates' messes, to break up the monotony and return the crew to a civilised way of life, if only for a few hours. The senior and junior rates in particular bonded and showed a sense of togetherness, with the junior rates serving the senior rates their food, then vice versa. It was the nearest the sub ever got to equality and a night off from the strict hierarchy that otherwise prevailed. Two or three of the crew had fathers and families who'd suffered in the recent miners' strike and, dessert over, they used to sing old pit songs that they'd grown up with as children. Poignantly, even though their families and way of life had been ravaged by the strike, they were the first in line when it came to serving their country, as was ever the case with British working-class communities.

The chefs excelled themselves for the mess dinner, pulling out all the stops and dishing up nothing less than the best: prawn cocktail to start, followed by fillet steak or beef Wellington, topped off with a baked Alaska or Black Forest gateau, all washed down with some of the finest Beaujolais, sherry and then port. The final chapter usually involved being carried to your bunk on a stretcher to sleep it off. Having been used to beer at sea for three months, the dinner could mean some seriously sore heads the following day, leaving many sailors a jibbering wreck. Thank Christ a lot of senior rates would volunteer to cover watches so we'd have recovery time in our racks before breakfast.

23

THE DAY JOB,
THE NIGHT JOB, REPEAT

On patrol, watch time consisted of me spending all my days in and around the control room as part of the tactical systems team, which in turn was part of the warfare team, the boat's fighting arm. The main aspect of the job was the interpretation of data fed through from either the sound room (sonar contacts) or periscopes (visual contacts made by the captain, XO or OOW at periscope depth). With all this data, it would then be possible to create a tactical picture for the skipper to use, figuring the course, speed and ranges off pretty much everything we came into contact with – the only exception being planes that we picked up on the electronic warfare (EW) equipment. In this instance there'd be no hanging around – all masts were immediately lowered and off we disappeared into the abyss, like a game of hide and seek, but with the added frisson of nuclear weapons.

My part in terms of helping to compile the tactical picture was five-fold: contact evaluation plot (CEP), local operations plot (LOP), fire-control system, periscope assistant and EW operator. Going into more detail, the CEP was a constantly rolling time-bearing plot in relation to our own ship's position, which was also plotted on the graph, highlighting our course and any changes we made. The plot was started as soon as we dived and finished the moment we surfaced. I sat in front of it, headphones on, which linked me through to the sonar guys in the sound room, who would update me every three to five minutes with the latest contacts they had on sonar. I'd then plot them against time on a chart that would also have a 360° area of location.

I'd plot all this on rolling graph paper that could be wound on by me, so it would show a plot of approximately two and a bit feet of ship sonar contacts at any one time. Its main purpose was to help the OOW work out rough courses of contacts, and then ultimately be used by the captain to work out and evaluate the complete tactical picture. Contacts were plotted and kept together by lines indicating target movements relative to us.

All contacts were assigned a contact number and were tracked until they were lost in the far distance or indeed they became so close that we had to alter course to keep safe. The basic principle of safety was that if a contact was moving to your left you'd want it on the port side of the boat, and if it was moving to your right you'd want it on the starboard side; it didn't matter even if it was a fast-moving contact because it would still be moving away from the boat. Things could get hairy when this principle was reversed; the contact might then be in a situation where it could have crossed our bow and collided. This would only have occurred at periscope depth if it was a ship contact. The nightmare scenario, however, was a fast-moving submarine contact moving left on our starboard side, coupled with uncertainty on our part as to the depth of the boat. That could have led to a serious collision.

In 2009, when HMS *Vanguard* was returning from patrol in the Atlantic Ocean, it collided with the French submarine *Le Triomphant*, causing an almighty shit-storm. Initially, the MOD denied that anything had happened, but it was subsequently forced to admit that a collision had indeed taken place while the boats had been dived. Substantial damage was inflicted on both boats, highlighting how inherently dangerous submarine operations can be.

Both of the submarines were nuclear powered, *Vanguard* being one of the Trident missile-carrying submarines that had replaced *Resolution* and her sister ships, while *Le Triomphant* was also equipped with nuclear missiles. Potential disaster was only avoided because of the slow pace at which both boats were travelling. The impact was still sizeable, and a report in the *Daily Telegraph* put the total bill for repair at £50 million. With both vessels covered in modern-day anechoic tiles and operating at slightly different depths, it's probable neither would have picked up on the other's sonar signature. If either of the submarines had been going at a faster speed the results might have been catastrophic for Britain, France and the whole of NATO.

The CEP allowed the plotter some artistic flair. After my initial removal during my first patrol I'd worked very hard and had become a very efficient operator. It wasn't Leonardo da Vinci, but I gave everything an individual flourish, with big, bold lines, classifications and course plotting. This was partly driven by boredom, as on any four-hour watch I might spend half the time on the plot with no contacts whatsoever. They tended to come in fits and starts – two hours might pass without any contacts, and then we might have four or five to deal with in quick succession. We'd try to fill the empty hours with jokes back and forth with the guys in the sound room or philosophical debate with my fellow watch-keepers in the control room. Who was worse, Stalin or Hitler? Is there life after death? Whose farts smelt worse, the coxswain's or the skipper's? These and various other questions were pondered, usually through the night watches, to alleviate our tiredness and overcome the tedium. Politics, however, was a no-go area – it would inevitably come round to the pros and cons of nuclear weapons, which seemed a bit pointless given we were 15 minutes from launching them.

Just behind the CEP lay the fire-control system. This was usually manned by three men on the attack team, but on patrol two men were left to manage (except when the submarine was returning to periscope depth, when it would be fully manned), plus the petty officer tactical systems (POTS); he would sit in the middle on an open line to the chief operating officer in the sound room discussing contacts and establishing which was the closest, a vital piece of information when coming up to periscope depth as the skipper needed to know where to focus when operating the periscope. Some captains liked to be told where the nearest contact was – 'Red 25', for example, meant the nearest ship contact was 25 degrees on his port bow.

The fire-control system was fairly state of the art for a late-1980s computerised firing set-up. In hindsight, it was like a computerised version of the CEP, with shit graphics where contacts looked more like human sperm bearing down on us from all directions. The contacts would be sent through from the sound room with their bearing and appear on the fire-control system, where we'd allocate them a target number (the same one as the CEP), so everyone knew which was which, and no cock-ups occurred.

Further details could then be entered into the system, such as how many propeller revs the contact was making as heard by the sound room. By the use of algorithms – yes, even 30 years ago the Royal Navy was well ahead of the technological curve – we could constantly update existing information to give us the target's best course, speed and range. It was particularly good when at periscope depth, as the skipper could pass on extremely accurate information and send a true bearing from the periscope onto the fire-control system. With that extra visibility we'd be able to get some seriously accurate data on contacts.

The fire-control system was powered by Ferranti computers and could track a large number of ships or submarines at any one time. It was considered the successor to all the manual plots, but it wasn't completely trusted as the sole provider of target information to the command. The manual plots, which could be tracked back in some form or other to the Second World War, were still the bread and butter of patrol life.

One plot that had become virtually extinct elsewhere was the LOP (local operations plot), which was situated aft of the fire-control system on the aft starboard side of the control room, on the nav plot table. It was the oldest of the manual plots still in use, and was particularly useful with fast-moving contacts as it gave a clear indication of how a target was behaving.

The last area I spent time in while watch-keeping was the electronic warfare shack, where the EW kit was kept. This helped detect radar transmissions from both surface and air contacts, and the strength of the signal would determine whether contacts were in a position where they could pick us up on their own radar. We'd try to see what operating band each individual contact was transmitting on and the type of signal it was sending out. Military vehicles tended to emit a different signal to a commercial airplane or ship.

Returning a submarine to periscope depth was probably the most dangerous manoeuvre we undertook. It was fraught with potential risks, mainly due to the change of depth and where the submarine surfaced; hopefully not under an oil tanker or similarly large vessel, which could rip the conning tower off and send everyone to the deep. The other main problem could be with an undetected submarine patrolling at a different depth, and if we changed our position it could lead to an underwater collision; unthinkable, but as HMS *Vanguard* proved, you never know.

Nearly all returns to periscope depth were for a BRN pass. This involved locking onto a satellite to get a highly accurate latitude and longitude bearing so we knew exactly where the boat was, which was necessary to determine the extent of our patrol area and ensure the accuracy of our missiles. For anti-detection purposes, periscope-depth excursions usually took place at night. The control room would be in black lighting and the blackout curtains were rigged up, with the passageway of 1 Deck so dark I felt as if I were blindfolded as I made my journey to the EW shack, careering off the side panels on my unsteady way.

The electronic warfare kit was inside another room set off the shack, tiny and compact. I'd sit down, switch it on and carry out pre-checks to make sure it was working properly, then wait with a certain amount of fear and adrenaline as the sub made the move back up to the shallows. I'd be listening in to the control room comms via the POTS, as the skipper ordered, 'Six up, keep 65 feet.'

The hulking 8,500-tonne boat would pitch quick as a Boeing 737 at the moment of take-off, seemingly weightless as the foreplanesman pulled back on his hand wheel and the aftplanesman pushed down on his to maintain the correct pitch of 6° up as the boat powered its way up to 65 feet, its set depth. Periodically, the chief ops came over the loud-speaker from the sound room, 'No contacts scanner, watcher clear,' shorthand for no close contacts were detected in the immediate vicinity on sonar. There was always the possibility of missing something altogether, but the conse-quences of that were best not talked – or even thought – about.

On passing 100 feet, the search periscope would be raised as the skipper got ready for action. It would also be time for everyone to stop talking unless asked a direct question by the captain or instructed to carry out one of his orders. Once the periscope broke through the water, he'd take an all-round look, first in low power, then another in high power, concentrating on where the POTS had indicated the nearest audible ship contact. He'd then ask for the electronic warfare mast to be raised. This was my moment of truth – hopefully it would be silent and I'd be looking at a blank display with no rackets.* Occasionally, the worst *did* happen and I'd pick up a contact. I could then judge the strength of that signal on our electronic warfare kit – above a certain strength, I'd be straight down the loudspeaker comms to the control room: 'Racket dangerous, racket dangerous, strength three.' The captain would then order, 'Down all masts,' and we'd be diving away to the deep.

---

* A racket is a contact picked up with the electronic warfare mast, usually a ship or aircraft radar.

If nothing was picked up, which was more the norm, especially on patrol, I'd sit there in the dark of the EW shack, monitoring the kit until our time at periscope depth was complete. On one patrol excursion to periscope depth I had a very strong contact, giving all the hallmarks of being a Soviet Tupolev Tu-142, a submarine-hunter aircraft with the NATO code name 'Bear'; we dived very quickly to the depths and didn't venture anywhere near periscope depth for around three weeks. It was normally very difficult to come up with a classification* in the very limited amount of time the boat was at periscope depth, but I felt it was always better to be safe than sorry, and the skipper was never going to get on our backs for being overly cautious with our classifications.

The EW shack was also one of the best hiding places on board to get away from everyone else, particularly at periscope depth. If I was on watch I could get an hour in there at the very least, time to switch on the equipment beforehand, then perform the system checks and powering down afterwards. It would break up the watch nicely and grab me some more valuable time on my own. The shack was also a space we used for recreation. Believe it or not, the EW kit was so sensitive that if it was switched on when we dived deep, it could pick up the BBC World Service or some other foreign stations, depending on where we were in the world.

---

* A classification in this instance refers to determining what type of aircraft or ship we had picked up on the EW kit.

In my present job I was once lucky enough to meet the legendary American boxer Sugar Ray Leonard while he was in the UK on a book-signing tour. I told him I'd tuned in to his infamous grudge fight with Marvin Hagler while ensconced in a steel tube deep under the ocean. He found it difficult to understand and gave me a pre-fight stare – either that, or he thought I was a complete tool. While underwater I also listened to Maradona's famous 'Hand of God' goal at the 1986 World Cup, the first time England and Argentina had played each other in any sporting capacity since the Falklands War, with Bryon Butler's wonderful commentary fading in and out as we changed course in the deep. It wasn't until I returned from patrol that I fully understood the significance of it.

It was mainly sporting events we tried to pick up, so we could relay the results to the rest of the guys in the boat. As well as the World Cup and Hagler vs Leonard, there were some other memorable moments, all picked up far below the waves, like the late, great and supremely talented Seve Ballesteros's extraordinary last round of 65 at the Open in 1988, Steffi Graf winning Wimbledon in 1988 on the way to the Grand Slam, Boris Becker retaining his Wimbledon title in the same year and England's calamitous showing at that year's European Championship. We'd also try to catch the football scores most Saturday evenings if at all possible; if not, at least my dad tended to send me some of them on a familygram.

It wasn't all sport, though. We'd try to tune into the World Service news to keep abreast of global events – Reagan and

Gorbachev held various summits while we were at sea, with Thatcher continuing her autocratic style of government. But it was disasters that kept my mind focused: the *Challenger* space shuttle tragedy, the Intifada that broke out in the occupied Palestinian territories, China's brutal repression of student demonstrations in Tiananmen Square, and the Troubles in Ireland (a long way from where we are today). The Chernobyl nuclear disaster was the most unnerving to us as a crew. A systems test had gone badly wrong, which led to the reactor massively overheating, followed by a series of explosions that released catastrophic radiation into the atmosphere, killing numerous emergency workers and civilians as a result. I remember being very upset about the accident, as were a lot of the crew. We knew the media were now going to be putting all of the UK's nuclear industry under the microscope – and there was none more news-worthy than the nuclear deterrent.

The general feeling on board was that our reactor was a lot easier – and indeed safer – to run and maintain than the one at Chernobyl, and that an accident was unthinkable and didn't bear contemplating. Nonetheless, the unthink-able could happen, and it was thanks to our highly trained, elite engineering team that everything ran smoothly. It still does.

The radio didn't only deliver sport and periodic bursts of gloom and doom, though. *Desert Island Discs* was a favourite, if we could have got to hear the bloody thing. I remember Michael Parkinson doing one with Kenneth

Williams as the castaway; it further opened my eyes to the world of classical music after listening to Schubert's Piano Trio No. 1. When I got back shore-side after patrol, I remember pouring half my wages on Brahms, Tchaikovsky, Barber, Mozart, Bach, Handel, Wagner, Strauss and Elgar.

At the systems console on the other side of the control room there was a tiny model of the sub – I think the chief wrecker had made it – sitting on a numbered scale, which would be pushed along a day at a time, which was somewhat disheartening; Day 1 complete, only another 80 to go. Whoever thought that was a good idea must have been a masochist. Every time I looked, it didn't appear to have moved, which just made everything worse.

Sitting on watch, I'd often think about us being cocooned in this undersea world, the extreme pressure of the water seemingly trying to crush the hull in this constant battle of extremes, us against the sea in one of the harshest of all man-made environments. It was quite normal for me to have feelings of impending disaster; sometimes I imagined the control room springing a leak and water gushing in so quickly we didn't have time to react, all hands lost to a watery grave. I always hoped if we did have some kind of life-threatening emergency that I would be fast asleep in my bunk, and death would be instantaneous and without drama. The deepest part of the Atlantic Ocean is nearly 28,000 feet deep, and the North Atlantic covers around 16 million square miles, so there's plenty of room for something to go wrong. At these operating depths, if something badly malfunctioned – loss of power, fire or flood – we would have had to ascend to the surface under emergency-blow conditions, whereby high-pressure air was forced into the ballast tanks to expel water, which in turn would dramatically lighten the boat so it could rise.

Before a submarine was able to surface like this, the OOW or captain would announce to the ship's company: 'Shut bulkhead doors, shut bulkhead doors, submarine surfacing in emergency.' Stopping loss of life was the first and only consideration. The command of 'Full ahead' would be given, the foreplanes whacking on a 10° bow up and the emergency tanks blowing us up there, the noise deafening as we launched ourselves out of the water after hitting the surface. On the flip side, if the emergency was a flood, with water pissing in everywhere, an emergency surface proce-dure might not have been possible, and a rushed escape would have been the only way to exit the submarine. Only those crew in the forward or aft escape hatches at either end of the boat would have managed to get out with the bulk-head doors shut, however. It wouldn't have mattered whether you were an officer or a rating – if you were in the middle of the boat, then it was game over. It was not some-thing I wanted to consciously dwell on, but precisely this scenario occasionally played itself out in one of my coffin dreams in my cramped bunk.

While still formal, relationships within the boat between officers and ratings were slightly less regimented than they were on surface ships, where a somewhat outdated approach to interpersonal skills tended to prevail, one that wouldn't have looked out of place in a Victorian workhouse. Bordering on condescension, it was widespread at the time I served and probably remains the same to this day. On submarines, however, due to the fact that you're cooped up with the same people for months on end – which can lead to tensions within the ranks – it tends to be different. We eschewed the military rigour of 'Yes, Sir, Yes, Sir, Three bags full, Sir' and used first names or nicknames for most of the crew, including the chief ops and the nuclear chief of the watch, aka 'Taff' and 'Smudge'. Officers were still addressed as 'Sir', but it wasn't like *Tom Brown's School Days*; instead it was affable and low-key. I could take the mickey, within reason – I'd never take the piss out of the captain or the XO; I didn't have a death wish – without it getting out of hand; it was always a laid-back but professional atmosphere while on watch in the control room. In many ways we were a boat of equals, with everyone fully aware that every person's job was as important as the next.

Most of my watches on board were under the command of the OOW, a seaman officer of varying degrees of experience – usually the TASO or the navigator. They were on the way to the ultimate test, the Perisher course, five to ten years further down the line. To pass, they required a keen knowledge of submarine operations, and while this was best gained playing hide and seek with the Soviets in a hunter-killer or diesel-boat environment, it was just as important to gain valuable experience on the nuclear deterrent to acquire the evasion techniques required to pass undetected for months on end.

They would work a one-in-three shift-pattern, and were de facto captains in charge of the sub while the skipper or XO got some shut-eye. All the captains I served with tended to be up at 7 a.m., and stayed awake right through till midnight – or else they'd catnap in the afternoon and be awake most of the night, with the XO working a slightly different pattern so they would complement each other. The captain had most of the main comms in his cabin, and one I served under used to scare the shit out of everyone in the control room by suddenly asking a question or querying an order at 2.30 a.m. I guess he was just keeping the crew on their toes. Although the OOW began every watch after completing a handover by saying, 'I have the submarine,' in reality he didn't; for the captain or XO could take it off him at any minute if they thought something were amiss, if we had to return to periscope depth or had a close sonar contact. In a case where the skipper was asleep and there was an emergency, the OOW couldn't afford to wait for him to get out of bed, so he would have to make life-and-death decisions and deal with the situation as best as he could.

24

LETTERS FROM THE GRAVE

When I kept watch in the control room out on patrol I used to sit quite near the safe where the 'letters of last resort' were kept. It always seemed surreal to me in many ways, having these documents so close by. My mind used to wonder just what was written in them. No one – not even the captain, the XO or the WEO – had any idea until they were opened. Luckily, to this day they never have been.

Only one person knew what was in them and that was the prime minister. Ever since the Royal Navy took over nuclear deterrence patrols, each PM* on assuming office had to write an identical letter to the four commanding officers of the deterrent, explaining what to do in the event of a nuclear strike devastating Britain that left the PM and his or her designated second choice, usually a senior cabinet member, incapacitated – or, more precisely, dead.

---

* The practice of writing 'letters of last resort' began with Ted Heath in the early 1970s. Although the nuclear deterrent began in 1968, the prime minister of the time, Harold Wilson, refused to write the letter.

Symbolically, this would be the last official act of HM Government.

During my service, given Britain and France's relatively small size compared with the other major nuclear states of the Soviet Union and US, in the event of a nuclear strike we were at a major geographical disadvantage; for while it might have taken a considerable number of strikes to obliterate the larger cities of the Soviet Union or the US, together with their armies, factories and buildings of state, a first-strike action from the Soviets could have wiped out all our government departments, Whitehall and the military–industrial complex, together with all our major conurbations.

Ten prime ministers have had to write these letters in the early days or weeks of assuming office. Former PMs are extremely reluctant to talk about such delicate security matters, and there's no mention of the letters in the memoirs of Thatcher, Major, Blair or Brown. I often speculated over their contents with fellow crewmates, but you had to be careful who you talked to, as some people were uncomfortable with making their feelings known on the matter and preferred to shut it out of their minds. Others who may have been against the use of the nukes also kept schtum, while some quite naturally could become quite tetchy as it would remind them of the unenviable job with which we'd been tasked.

The only people who did voice their opinions were the hardliners ('hangers and floggers', as I called them), who would simply say, 'Nuke the bastards!' It's thought, although it cannot be proven, that the options were/are: retaliate with the warheads; do nothing (brilliant); leave it to the captain; put the boat under the control of an ally (in our case the US); or try to save the boat by going to another part of the world, such as Australia or New Zealand. My personal preference would have been for the captain to save the crew and seek a safe haven, preferably in the Maldives or the Seychelles. It made the days pass more quickly idly thinking about the boat laying anchor off Reethi Beach, then swimming ashore to be met by five-star service, food and surf. I could but dream.

What we did worry about, though, was how we would save ourselves if things got so bad that we were marooned in the oceans, unsure what action to take. We would then have been subject to the biggest submarine hunt in history, furtively traversing the deep in an attempt to escape marauding Soviet naval forces, who by this time had developed a nuclear depth bomb. We would have been effectively signing our own death warrant if we'd launched our missiles, as enemy satellite equipment could have clearly picked up the submarine's position and it would have been just a matter of time before we were hunted down.

My time on board *Resolution* coincided with Thatcher being in Number 10, so I can imagine her letters might have gone for option one, immediate nuclear retaliation. After all, she'd already won a general election by going to war over the Falkland Islands. I used to hope that retaliation would have been deemed pointless by this stage, as most of the casualties of nuclear confrontation would be civilians and by then, with Britain already obliterated, what would have been the purpose? It seemed like madness, given that the Americans would have already launched God knows what by this point.

Hidden away in the depths of the oceans, how would we have known what was going on and whether events had reached such a terminal impasse if we didn't communicate? One way would have been to monitor communications from Submarine Command in Northwood, and if these ceased for four hours or more – not exactly a long time – then the letters could be opened. Another option was if the BBC's Radio 4 or World Service (both of which I was able to pick up in the EW room on the warfare kit) had stopped broadcasting; in which instance I would have been the boat's harbinger of doom. It would have been highly unlikely for a nuclear strike to come straight out of the blue, and besides, it's almost certain we would have been on patrol with heightened military tensions at the very least, or more likely, we'd already have been in a state of war with the Soviets and the Warsaw Pact.

25

CAPTAIN IS GOD

The captain is the boss, pure and simple. I can't think of a single job in any other branch of the military that's as stressful or important as the captain of the nuclear deterrent. The responsibility is awesome. It's his decision, and his alone, whether we launch our missiles according to the contents of the letters of last resort. Imagine accepting responsibility for such incomprehensible destruction.

During my submarine career I served under three captains, all of whom, though markedly different in their approach and outlook, possessed great authority and were treated with almost God-like reverence by the rest of the crew. The captain of a Polaris submarine was usually an experienced submarine commander with a couple of commands under his belt before he was given the ultimate job, which could be a fairly lonely and exceedingly stressful post. But most of them thrived on the responsibility of being potentially the last man standing in the UK's chain of command and having to face the ultimate decision – whether or not to launch nuclear weapons. The captain could have no doubts about the job that was required, no question about what was expected, nor could he waver if required to launch the missiles.

The skills that had taken the captain to this point would have been gained over roughly a decade as a seaman officer, followed by the decisive test of all prospective submarine commanders, the Submarine Command Course, aka the Perisher (so-called because you either pass or perish). Established in 1917, the course is still run over a hundred years later, on virtually the same principles: whether a candidate is fit to take a submarine to war and all that this entails, but also fit to be in charge of a ship's company while keeping the submarine safe in the most pressurised of environments. Back when I was serving, the ten prospective captains on the course were divided into two separate classes, headed up by two serving commanding officers known as Teachers. There were usually two courses a year, one starting in summer and one in November. Lasting about four months, the course was the toughest leadership test in the British military – nothing else came close. There was a 25 to 30 per cent fail rate among the candidates, which meant one in every four people who attempted the Perisher would find themselves forbidden to return to sea on a submarine.*

---

* This is different nowadays. The course is much smaller. There is only one Teacher and the class sizes vary. It is also less brutal. If it looks as if you might fail, Teacher can remove you from the course and allow you to take it again next time around. The Submarine Service is now so small that it can't afford to lose highly-trained officers.

The first part of the course was simulation-based, taking place either at Faslane or at Plymouth, mixed with some theory. The candidates were eased into the programme with the running of dummy attacks against a single warship as they prepared for the sea phase of the course. This usually lasted about two months, with the most severe test coming during the last month. It was at that point that most of the fails occurred, with the majority coming in the final week – and how brutally instant and final they were. Candidates had been failed on the last day, feeling they'd done enough to get through, only to be told by Teacher they hadn't quite got what it took to make the grade. In that instance the submarine would surface, then the candidate was told his fate, given a bottle of whisky to drown his sorrows, led off the boat to an awaiting transfer vessel and taken back to shore, never to set foot on a submarine again. Perisher failure meant no longer serving in the Submarine Service. A career on surface ships or leaving the service altogether were really the only options left. It was shit or bust, highlighting the importance of the position everyone was striving for.

The final sea phase was by far the toughest. A Royal Navy nuclear submarine was used in permanent rotation as the Perisher examination boat and could go to sea with its usual crew, captain and XO included, supplemented by Teacher and the candidates. During the final phase, the candidates were expected to undertake intelligence gathering or minelaying, simulated from the torpedo tubes, with minelaying testing in particular the candidate's navigational skills when operating close to inshore coastlines.

The main part of the final phase, though, was evading and attacking up to three frigates around the Isle of Arran. The main point of this was to see whether the candidate could keep the submarine and its crew safe, as well as being able to launch any simulated attacks on the enemy boats. He had an imaginary safety circle around the boat, usually at around 1,000 yards, called the 'go deep' circle. If any of the frigates came within that radius, he had to be able to evade by diving the boat and listening to the sounds of the propellers going past overhead. If he evaded too soon, Teacher may have felt he was being overly cautious and was not quite up to the job; leaving it too late could result in a collision as the passing frigate overhead lopped the top off the conning tower. Not good.

Each candidate had to work out the course, speed and range of each of the frigates, and calculate the duration of his 'look interval', the time in which he could safely raise the periscope to keep an eye on each of the frigates before they entered his go deep circle and he needed to lower the periscope and dive to avoid the risk of collision. He might, for example, have had 40 seconds to look at the other two frigates before the first ship entered the go-deep circle. Because the distance between him and the enemy vessels constantly expanded and contracted during the attack, he needed to ensure none of the three vessels had changed speed or, more dangerously, changed their course towards the submarine.

What usually happened was that two frigates jousted with the perimeter of the go-deep circle, while the third frigate came through the middle at top speed, heading straight for the submarine. Any one of them could have changed direction at any time, and it was up to the candidate to judge when and if he needed to take evasive action – or undertake an attack. It was certainly not for the faint-hearted, and just to throw a spanner in the works, a crew member would be told to have a psychotic episode in the control room or a mechanic to rush in with an imaginary finger missing, all to ratchet up the pressure. At the same time, emergencies would be happening on the boat: fires, floods, hydraulic bursts, the works. To pass all of this, the candidates had to show the three basic principles of submarine command: leadership of the boat and crew; operations including attacks, navigation and minelaying; and finally, being safely in charge of the boat and its crew in any scenario dreamt up by Teacher. The course was a constant test of nerve and aptitude, but the rewards were career-defining.

My first skipper was Commander Thompson, an old-fashioned toff and a real public-school type – I can't remember whether it was Eton, Harrow or Winchester – whose family, it was rumoured, were landed gentry and owned half of Yorkshire. I guess it was just written in the stars that he'd make it to admiral by the end of his career. He kept himself to himself and didn't encourage conversation, especially with a Part 3 lowlife like myself, just starting out and striving for his dolphins. I remember once I was operating the CEP* in the control room on my first patrol. It could get fairly hectic, and neatness was essential in order to give the command a broad picture of what was going on tactically. He took one look at it, then whispered something to the OOW, and within five minutes I was removed from the plot. It was very embarrassing for me – not at all what I wanted to hear – and being so young it was pretty hard to take in. My confidence shot to pieces, I was very wary of him from that day on.

He'd smoothly float his way around the boat and had this habit of appearing just when you'd least expect it, right there, face first – and of course I'd immediately become a jibbering wreck. The crew respected him, as I did, although I'm not sure they warmed to him. I suspect he was supremely unconcerned by that. He personified the 'them and us' culture rife in the British military at that time – and still today – reproducing all that was wrong in society as a whole, in as much as you could immediately pinpoint someone's rank by the way they spoke. It was a great rarity to hear an officer with a neutral accent.

The captain's behaviour would be mimicked all the way down the rest of the group, and before long you'd have a 'You should know your place' attitude being endorsed, which in certain circumstances – not all – could lead to a person being judged on their background not their ability. In my experience there were many senior and junior rates who

---

* Contact evaluation plot.

were at least the equal of most of the officers on board. While there have been submarine captains who've come right up through the ranks – and hats off to them, for they must be seriously capable – it's still a very small percentage.

I remember once going on board an American sub that was visiting Faslane. I found the crew to be a much more harmonious group of sailors, in terms of how the officers and men interacted; more a reflection of, say, the Midwest or Upstate New York rather than the hide-bound, provincial, class-structured ways of post-war Britain, in which one's social class was all that mattered. To a great extent the public schools are to blame, as the officer classes – the 'Ruperts', as we came to know them – have been groomed on their playing fields for centuries. I met a lot of officers during my service who couldn't understand why I'd joined the rank and file, as I'd gone to public school. I had officer papers 'raised' on me when I was on subs, which meant someone was keen to see me packed off to Dartmouth for officer training, but I was never in the slightest bit interested. I enjoyed my time in the ranks, and wouldn't have swapped it for the world. It was a real in-depth look at the workings of these boats and the men who served on them, whereas being an officer gave you a much narrower view of what actually happened at sea. When it came down to it, the boat was run by the leading hands on board – the head junior rates. They ensured that everything ticked over, the jobs got done and discipline remained sound. The senior rates, who made certain that every department ran like clockwork, only got involved if someone was not pulling their weight and needed a kick up the arse.

My next captain, Commander Brown, was a breath of fresh air in terms of his approach to the ship's company. A far more engaging, dynamic and friendly face, he seemed genuinely concerned with bringing the crew together, and spent much time visiting the junior and senior rates' messes. He was also married to a Wren (Women's Royal Naval Service), so had an appreciation of some of the subtler aspects of Navy life. Having served as captain on a diesel submarine and also skippered a hunter-killer S-class boat, his formative years of command had been spent charging madly around the Atlantic and further afield, chasing Soviet submarines, conducting intelligence gathering operations, under-the-ice excursions and Special Forces drops. He was a skipper at the top of his game, but he also possessed a close affinity to the crew, determined as he was to create a tighter, more cohesive group.

He had a side to him, though. Woe betide you if you overstepped the mark and became overfamiliar with him; he'd cut you to the bone with a simple stare or a raised eyebrow – imagine having Roger Moore as skipper. He told great stories about the people he'd worked with, like the first captain he'd served under, who used to bound into the control room every night dressed in a nightshirt and night-cap like Ebenezer Scrooge in *A Christmas Carol*, before retiring to his cabin swinging off the pipes – a total eccentric.

I remember Brown saying sorry for a miscommunication to one of the wreckers as we were levelling off after diving. The wrecker then made a joke, and the skipper simply looked at him and said, 'You've caught me on a good day but let's get one thing clear. I don't do apologies.' The guy nearly dropped off his chair as the skipper's eyes bored into him. Not the best course of action, getting on the wrong side of the big man on the first dive on his first patrol in command.

When Brown was in his cabin and most of us thought him asleep, he would regularly monitor the communications throughout the rest of the boat and often chip in with, 'This is the captain,' followed by a statement or question that would leave everyone flummoxed. A stickler for correct communications, while also being something of a rebel, he could shift from having a friendly conversation with you one moment to giving you a bollocking the next, but he didn't hold grudges. He was a captain very much from the direct-answer brigade; you made sure you gave him a direct answer whether he liked it or not, no flannel or waffle – just the truth. As the most popular and interesting captain I served under, we were very chuffed indeed when, just before he left the boat, he told us we were the best and most professional crew he had served with during his career, although I bet he said that to all his crews.

My final captain was Commander Johnson, a ferociously intelligent man from an engineering background who had obviously applied these principles to being a seaman officer. Captaining a submarine requires a highly mathematical and logical brain in order to quickly evaluate the tactical picture, both at depth and – even more so – at periscope depth, where you need to work out how quickly vessels are closing against how fast the submarine is going, plus being able to look through the periscope at safe intervals without compromising the safety of the crew or the boat's whereabouts. A master of all of this, he was both solid and dependable, and while perhaps lacking the flair and charisma of Brown or the self-confidence of Thompson, he was an extremely able commanding officer.

He was very cool with me in a final meeting I had before leaving the Navy. We talked at great length about the five and a bit years I'd spent in the service, but he also took a passing interest in my full name. 'Richard Patrick Valentine Humphreys?' he said. 'Christ, with a name like that you should be standing here instead of me.'

26

TO LAUNCH OR
NOT TO LAUNCH

The greater part of patrol life centred around our ability to unleash nuclear weapons on the Soviets at 15 minutes' notice, should Britain find herself subjected to a nuclear attack. The deterrent would only be used as a second-strike option, but in the days of the Cold War the perception of the public at large was that we were teetering on the edge of nuclear destruction. Cold War brinkmanship, spying, propaganda and the rise of hawks on the right, both in the UK and in the States, with Thatcher and Ronald Reagan (who'd succeeded ex-submariner Jimmy Carter), had led to increased tension between East and West. This continued into the 1980s, and by the end of the decade the threat of all-out nuclear confrontation had escalated and was never far from the headlines. Nowhere was this felt more acutely than on board my submarine.

We practised a firing drill at least once a week. During this exercise we'd receive the firing signal from fleet headquarters at Northwood, and a pipe would go over the main broadcast: 'XO WEO wireless office.' They'd both haul themselves along to the radio shack as quickly as possible, where they'd rip off a coded message from Submarine Command, then make their way back to the control room where the message was decoded using code books locked away inside a double safe. This authentication message would be matched against codes. It was then the captain's responsibility to check whether the signal was the real thing or an exercise. No one person could launch the missiles singlehandedly; a series of steps – a checklist, if you like – was followed whereby different crew members' responsibilities had to be fulfilled and ticked off, before the next step could be actioned and the launch continued. Once authenticated, the submarine was brought to action stations for missile launch.

The WEO would leave the control room via the aft ladder, go to the missile control centre on 3 Deck to spin up the missiles ready for launch, check the guidance codes and stand by with the old-fashioned firing mechanism. It looked like the grip of a handgun, with a trigger that would actually commence the firing sequence and propel the missiles out of the tubes and away to their targets. With the WEO safely tucked away in the missile control centre, the submarine made its way to launch depth. And then the fun began.

The pitch of the submarine first had to be perfect. In order to launch the missiles, this 8,500-tonne, 20th-century man-of-war needed to be able to hover completely still to launch its grim payload into the skies. The hover pump was controlled at the systems console, and either let water in or out, pumping or flooding to maintain launch depth. The submarine slowed right down, and adjustments were made to any bubble buoyancy issues with a tweak of the afterplanes and foreplanes, all of which helped keep the submarine level and ready for action.

Behind the periscopes, sitting on the outside of the nav centre, was the attack centre info panel, a light indicator console that illuminated the status of the individual missiles. The captain's key went into the bottom of this. When we were safely at depth, hovering nicely, he would turn the key and announce over the loudspeaker system: 'The WEO has my permission to fire.' Upon hearing this, the missiles would be spun in a pre-determined sequence and then fired by the WEO. A high-pressure pump forced gas into the tube, opening the missile hatch and propelling the missile out and upwards as it headed towards the surface, finally breaking through to the world above.

The missile at this point stopped dead in its tracks for what seemed an eternity, but was actually less than a second, before the rocket motor ignition kicked in with a mighty roar. It now essentially became a rocket, albeit a massively armed one, and launched into outer space on a pre-determined flight path, homing in on its target via a high-arcing orbit. The missile could be guided by the boat's computers or become self-guided, should the boat come under attack, and would fly towards its target following re-entry from space. After second-stage ignition, the decoys would launch, teasing Moscow's air defences, and somewhere in all the chaos the actual warhead would sneak through, cleverly hidden, stealthily homing in on its target with devastating effect.

Of course, none of this happened, thank Christ. We only ever completed these drills as part of a weapons systems readiness test, and when the signal was decoded it immediately became clear that this was just an exercise, not the real thing. We practised again and again until it became second nature and everyone was suffering from the extreme tedium of it all. The world could have ended, and we would each one of us have been bored fartless doing it.

Seriously, though, what would have been the reaction had the firing signal come through? I've got no hesitation in saying it would have been carried out, the crew doing their job as professionally as possible. I shudder to think what I would have done afterwards – gone and wept in my bunk, I guess. Britain as a country would have been wiped out; family, friends and loved ones dead, much of the so-called civilised world completely flattened. And for what? To kill all of them, as they'd killed us? Nothing could have brought back the dead, and the deterrent would have been proved worthless, having failed in its basic purpose – to preserve the peace.

I remember listening to a WEO on one of those TV news items on the nuclear deterrent that used to pop up from time to time, wittering on about how he'd have found it more of an honour than a burden to pull the trigger. I'm presuming the poor man lost all clarity of thought with the

TV lights and cameras on him. I can't remember serving with anyone who'd have found it 'an honour' to help precipitate such an unthinkable cataclysm.

What I am quite sure of is that having the deterrent for the last 50 years has made the possibility of nuclear conflict almost non-existent. I, and many of the crew I served with, believed whole-heartedly we would never receive the firing signal. I couldn't think of any circumstances in which it would have come through; it would simply never have happened. I went through my whole career taking this for granted. It made everything more bearable, especially as I ate, slept, drank, showered and kept watch no more than 100 feet away from the most powerful weapon Britain had ever produced.

It became a mental battle of will every time I heard the phrase 'XO WEO wireless office', but I always believed it would be a signal for another drill. Who was going to take the decision to destroy their own country, a country that had suffered great hardship from the time of the tsars, through the Bolshevik Revolution, to the Great Terror and the famines of Stalin's premiership, during which an estimated 10 to 20 million Soviets perished, not to mention the Second World War, which accounted for a further 26 million lives? The Soviets would never have undertaken a first-strike option. What was in it for them? Not even Kremlin hardliners would have contemplated ritual suicide.

During the Cold War neither side was prepared to take a step back, and this lack of trust fuelled paranoia and led to a preposterous build-up of both their nuclear arsenals. They were now in the business of MAD – mutually assured destruction – and this was the game that I was in. The more deadly the weaponry became, the less likely the confrontation. I saw nuclear weapons as an incessant and unremitting threat, but never a *real* one, as no one was willing to play the ultimate game.

Even though nuclear war remains a very distant possibility, our weapons have hardly made the world a more peaceful or safer place. Since the deterrent patrols began, Britain has been embroiled in wars both at home and abroad: the Troubles in Northern Ireland, the Falklands War of 1982, the First Gulf War of 1990–91, the Bosnian War of the early 1990s and the Kosovo War of 1998–99, wars in Afghanistan and Iraq, the fight against Islamic State … the list is considerable. What all these interventions have taught us is that our having the nuclear deterrent has not been enough to keep the peace. Conventional warfare continues regardless of who the nuclear states are.

Over the last 20 years we've become entangled in wars in faraway places, which in turn have been responsible for stoking the fires of radical Islamism in this country. The world's nuclear powers stood by helplessly as first Saddam Hussein, then Bashar al-Assad used chemical weapons on their own populations, Western military might in neither case acting as a deterrent. The same can be said about the annexation of Crimea in 2014 and the attempted assassination of a Russian double agent and his daughter in Salisbury in 2018; Russian leader Vladimir Putin, who ordered the first and is alleged to have been behind the second, knows he can act with impunity, as he also possesses nuclear weapons. Meanwhile, we seem to have no hesitation in spending anything up to £31 billion, with an extra £10 billion in reserve – apparently the going price to deter the ultimate confrontation – on four new submarines to replace Trident in ten to fifteen years' time. Some argue that our nuclear obsession is more to do with perceived power, and that our place at the top table, a hangover from the bygone days of empire, is only ensured by maintaining the deterrent. It's all well and good believing that, especially when it's not your responsibility to launch the missiles.

27

HOMEWARD BOUND

The last week on board was always quite a tense affair, as everyone had endured a belly-full of living underwater by week ten or so, and it was time to get back. By then, we were sick of the routine – and sick of each other. I always tried to keep myself to myself in those final couple of weeks, to avoid any flashpoints with short-tempered crewmates who just wanted to get back to their wives or girlfriends.

The boat would now become even more claustrophobic than it was when we first dived. I could cope quite well initially with the routine of watch-keeping, eating, movies and self-study, but the further into the patrol cycle we went, the more oppressive it became. Time really seemed to slow down, the walls appeared to be closing in on me, my bunk felt smaller, the living quarters on 3 Deck looked like they'd shrunk and there was no room to walk in the passageways. Ten weeks without fresh air and sunlight were finally taking their toll. Once the signal had been received that the boat and crew relieving us had reached their diving area, had submerged and were bedded into their patrol area, it was time for us to re-enter the land of the living.

Patrol end was completed by surfacing the boat, nearly always in the Atlantic off the coast of Ireland, then we'd head back to Coulport to unload the missiles before returning to base at Faslane the following day. I usually experienced a sense of relief, mixed with a tinge of sadness, when we surfaced. By week four or five I'd got used to the sweaty stench, and although I'd banged my head on pipes and slipped down stairwells, I'd also watched some great movies (and some dodgy porn), eaten some fantastic food (under the circumstances), coped with sleeping in a coffin and dealt with the relentless heat. Now it was time to give it all up and return to normal life – yet a part of me didn't want to. As grim as it could be, there were so many moments that made it all worthwhile, and the camaraderie was impossible to replace.

The submarine would first glide up to periscope depth, where the captain would make a prolonged, all-round sweep on the periscope. Once happy, he would give the XO the order to surface, which involved blowing the ballast tanks – the forward first, followed by the aft – with highly compressed air to expel the water within them. Our black leviathan then ascended bow first. Blowing water out from its tanks, the boat emitted more noise than it had made since first diving all those weeks ago. A rise on the fore-planes saw the boat breach the surface, the ballast tanks full of air and the boat's density less than the water outside; this is known as positive buoyancy, with the boat staying on the surface. The captain remained on the periscope all through the procedure to check he was happy with how the boat was lying in the water before he ordered the conning tower hatches to be opened. When he was satisfied, he'd order, 'On the surface, open up.'

With this, the conning tower lower lid was slowly opened by the OOW, shadowed by the lookouts as they prepared to go up the conning tower to guide the boat back into port. Once the lower lid was open, the OOW would then climb up to unclip the upper lid, which again he'd open very slowly as an airtight vacuum had been created all the time we'd been down on patrol. The air would gush in as the upper lid opened, making quite a din – but worse was to follow. The smell of rotten fish, created by the build-up of algae and saltwater in the casing, would seep into the control room, making me gag.

I looked forward to surfacing immensely, especially the times when I was chosen to be one of the lookouts, which happened on a couple of patrols. It was a surreal sight being second up the conning tower and part of the first team onto the bridge. Standing there, the fishy stench offset by the fresh air, I was always completely speechless as I took in the never-ending vista of the Atlantic. Only an hour before I'd been in the cramped depths of the ocean below, and now here I was, standing up top, drinking huge gulps of fresh air down into my lungs, getting high on it after weeks of breathing in only recycled air, food, machinery smells and other men's body odour. It was the best feeling in the world, with my eyes trying to refocus on the limitless expanse of sky and sea stretched out in every direction. For the past three months I'd been focusing no more than 30 feet in front of me.

As HMS *Resolution* ploughed through the water, a considerable snowy-white wake formed behind her like the jet trail of a plane; seawater, blown in my face by the wind, stung and refreshed my skin, while the sun beat down, drenching me with hard-earned vitamin D. During these two days of coming back to port, I spent as much time as I could keeping watch on the bridge, soaking up the rays and trying to adjust to whatever normality might have in store for me.

It was also a time to count your blessings – not so much the joy of coming home, more the sense of relief that no disasters had occurred and we'd survived without any great dramas. Now was the chance to relax and enjoy the long way back. Not surprisingly, the journeys home were always far more jovial than the hard slogs to patrol area. This final homecoming was without fanfare, unheralded, almost sheepish, as this monster of menace drifted back into Coulport after another visit to the deep. Armageddon would be offloaded at the depot, then it was a swift trip back to Faslane, with friends and family ensconced on the Rhu Narrows, the entrance to Gare Loch, waving to us from the shore as we sailed past. They would have been told of our arrival 24 hours earlier, to give them enough time, if they so wished, to make it up to Scotland.

As we approached port there would always be a welcoming party standing there in salute. They'd come on board to greet us, and there was usually some high-ranking admiral or other who'd look down his nose at us, accompanied by his hangers-on. I felt like telling them to bugger off, particularly as we'd been away for 90 days and had to clean the boat from top to bottom to make everything spick and span for them. I'm sure they were appalled at the rag-tag, pasty appearance of us all. A VIP of some description would usually be rolled out to join us every time we returned from patrol; why we couldn't come back on our own as a unit, I simply don't know. On one occasion Prince Charles jumped aboard; he took an interest in everyone's welfare and asked some pertinent questions about life on board, which came as a surprise.

We'd done our bit to keep the country safe. A lot has been written about other branches of the armed forces over the last 20 years, but nothing about the self-sacrifice of the brave men – and now women – who made up the crews of the nuclear deterrent. Direct military action it certainly wasn't, but the stresses and strains of anything up to 12 weeks underwater were mentally, spiritually and emotionally difficult to comprehend when I first started, but now for me had become a normal way of life.

* * *

In total, HMS *Resolution* was to undertake 61 deterrent patrols, the most of any of the Polaris fleet, and I was on around 10 per cent of these. *Renown*, *Repulse* and *Revenge* would carry out a further 168 patrols, so between 1968 and

1996, when Polaris was finally replaced by the even more powerful Trident boats with their longer-range missiles, 229 patrols were carried out, through all of which the boats remained undetected. This figure has moved to over 350 patrols for the deterrent as of January 2019.

John Major, prime minister at the time, said this after HMS *Repulse* completed the last Polaris patrol in 1996:

> We are here today to pay tribute to the work of the Polaris Force. The debt we owe is very large. For the last 28 years, this Force has mounted continuous patrols that have been vital to ensure this country's peace and security. Because of these patrols, any possible aggressor has known that to attack the UK would provoke a terrible response.
>
> In particular, we are here today to pay tribute to the last of the four Polaris submarines, HMS *Repulse*, which returned from her sixtieth and final deployment in May. But not only *Repulse*, of course. I pay tribute, too, to the other three boats and their crews in her Class: the *Resolution* herself, *Renown* and *Revenge*. Each has made its own unique and invaluable contribution to the remarkable record of maintaining a Polaris submarine at sea, on deterrent patrol, undetected by friend or foe, every day, of every year, from 1969 until May this year.

28

OFF CREW

Coming back alongside in later patrols, I usually found myself perched on the bridge with the navigator, captain, XO, VIP and lookouts. It would be a tight squeeze but was certainly worth it, as *Resolution* cruised cocksure of herself up Gare Loch and then, with the help of tugs, was expertly manoeuvred back to the jetty where she'd be laid up in prime position, posing at the front of the jetty. Although I'd become very attached to her after nigh on three months under the sea, it would now be time to descend into the bowels of the boat before the remaining stores were offloaded by the crew, which could take a while. When *Resolution* returned from her record-breaking 108-day patrol in 1991, the rumour going round was that the only food left on board was removed from the boat in a half-empty black bin-liner.

Offloading complete, my kit would be gathered up in a small grip bag and off we'd go, the Port crew waiting for us up on the jetty. The pasty, stinking, sweaty masses of the Starboard crew filed out past them with a smile and a wink

– 'All yours now. See you in three months,' then onto the jetty and back to our rooms on the base for the longest hot bath in Christendom, with fresh soap and shampoo. On stepping out of the bath, the water would have the colour and smell of a fetid, stagnant pond, the stench that had collected within my pores finally released after 12 weeks and now sluicing off down the plughole. Most of the married guys tended to head off home straight away; us single guys would have a night out in Helensburgh.

It doesn't require much imagination to picture what form these first nights back from patrol took. First of all there'd be a carb-heavy dinner and a couple of pints at the base, then a taxi at the main gates would run us into Helensburgh for the start of the carnage. The evening would commence at the Imps (the Imperial Hotel), where the booze flowed constantly. Everyone was jovial and there were never any violent undertones – we just wanted a laugh, to let ourselves go after months under the sea. The doctor led the charge around various pubs – The Royal, The Cavalier, Bar L – and then on to a club if we could still find one that would let us in, as by this point we'd be fairly well inebriated. It was here that the heavy drinking, the shirts off and the dancing on tables commenced – all in good jest – as we sang and bawled our way through to the early hours. The night would end in one of two ways: in a cab heading back to the flat of a young woman who'd taken pity on me and my dreadful dance moves in the club, or, more than likely, to the Akash Tandoori up the road for more food and dodgy cheap wine.

Then we'd pack into a fast black cab and head back to the base, windows down in case anyone had an attack of the Big Vom – or sometimes worse; leakage was possible from literally any orifice, depending on how far gone we were. Once I clambered out of a cab just as my mate hit the punchline of a joke. I laughed so hard I managed to follow through as my leading foot struck the pavement. Embarrassing, to put it mildly, as I clenched my bum cheeks together, gingerly making my way back to my rooms, the emergency hand-washing of my jeans immediately commencing. Or we'd get in and do the old 'light a fart with a lighter' routine, seeing how far the flame would go, although this usually ended up with someone setting fire to their bedclothes, clothing or, even more painfully, their sphincter. It was quite literally like a Wild West show as Helensburgh was subjected to a series of nights of drunken debauchery by returning submarine crews on their first nights home, with alcohol and sex readily available.

'Off crew', as we called this break, was great as we could do pretty much anything we liked for about three or four weeks. Obviously, I'd spend time with family and friends, and occasionally I'd go back to Wolverhampton to see old schoolmates, although I found myself increasingly distant from them as time passed, probably because our lives were so different to how they'd been three or four years earlier. I still loved them, though; I was just too immature to express it correctly.

Patrols were also a good way of saving up cash, as there's not much call for spending under the ocean. Apart from settling my canteen bill when I got back shore-side, it usually meant there was enough money left to enjoy a holiday, usually somewhere hot and not too far – the Canary Islands or southern Spain did the trick. On one patrol, I developed a horrendous rash over my torso called *Pityriasis rosea*. Mainly caused by stress and anxiety, both of which were a given when away in the deep, my body looked like a seething mass of raised scaly red patches; the *Singing Detective* had come back to haunt me big time.

A week in Tenerife in over 30°C-degree heat sorted me out. On the beach every day, Robert Graves's *Goodbye to All That* in hand, lying on some rocks with a towel, taking long swims in the warm and glittering Atlantic Ocean, it was all a world away from the deep, freezing swells of the North Atlantic that I was used to. I did this for seven days solid, and I must have been a total bore to my fellow crewmates I'd gone away with. But I didn't care – I'd had enough of all of them by this time and needed some valuable time on my own to unwind from the stresses and strains that had caused me to look like I did. A week later, I returned to the glorious west coast of Scotland, feeling cured, refreshed and with a deep tan, the healthiest I'd looked in five years.

Ibiza was another hangout we escaped to. I recently returned there for work and then for my honeymoon the following year, but didn't recognise it, so much had changed from the end of the 1980s. There was much more of a hippie vibe then, but now the club scene was up and running, with DJs jetting in from mainland Europe. At the end of the 80s, hedonism ran riot, and alcohol and weed were the order of the day as we revved it up in Ku, Amnesia and Pacha in baggy shirts and trousers, wearing multi-coloured bandanas. I'm not sure the Navy would have approved.

On another off crew, three of us decided to go travelling around Europe. Me and Jim knew each other pretty well, but Rod, the third guy, we didn't really know at all as he hadn't been on the boat very long. He'd been a fisherman from Norfolk coastal stock, spending long spells away in the North Sea; this tough and uncompromising way of life for someone so young meant he was ideally suited to the mental stresses and strains of submarines. We arranged to go the week after seeing our friends and relatives, for what we hoped would be three cool weeks inter-railing round the continent, taking in some of the cultural highlights. We planned to meet at Glasgow Central Station the following Sunday, but things got off to a bad start when Jim turned up on the Saturday, thought we weren't showing up and headed off under his own steam down to the coast and took the ferry to France. With that, he was away, as there was no way of contacting him pre-mobile phones.

Rod and I proceeded to board the train from Glasgow to London, and I prepared to get some kip before we hit the capital. Rod had other ideas. Off he popped to the on-board restaurant and came back with two bacon rolls and 24 cans of Heineken. Not cool. I knew he was a heavy drinker, but this set the alarm bells ringing. His bender started in

Amsterdam and continued for three days without a break. I wanted to have some nice food, smoke some weed and then perhaps see the Rijksmuseum, Van Gogh Museum, Rembrandt House Museum, Anne Frank's house, then go to the De Meer Stadion, the home of Ajax, as I'd been obsessed by Cruyff, Neeskens and Ruud Krol as a kid and wanted to go and watch a game. But no, Rod wanted to go to the red-light district and screw prostitutes. We never actually made it there, as we went out for a drink in some dive bar nearby where he proceeded to get paralytic, and we had to get out of there quickly before we both got a hiding from the locals.

This became the norm as we headed around mainland Europe – in fact we were nearly murdered in a strip-show in Vienna. I'd grabbed some time on my own and after a trip round the Belvedere, once the home of Prince Eugene of Savoy in the Habsburg's imperial capital, we proceeded to ensconce ourselves in a sex club in one of the seedier parts of the city. A brunette – and a dead ringer for Susanna Hoffs – slid up to me and offered herself: £90 for 20 minutes. Jesus, I wasn't paying that, even for a member of The Bangles. Rod, of course, was still recovering from a hangover from the night before, and the seven before that, and had come out without his wallet. The Eastern European gangsters who owned the place were circling, insisting we had to pay for something, otherwise we'd be in trouble. So, two drinks it was, plus a live sex show. Fifty quid lighter, we made haste into the Viennese moonlight.

The next morning, fretful, depressed and with no end in sight to the holiday from hell, I ate a hearty breakfast, packed my rucksack, left Rod asleep and got the first train out of there heading directly west, to Munich, where I had a great time staying with a German family as I spoke a bit of the lingo. While I was staying here the Berlin Wall came down, followed by a party that lasted three days non-stop.

But it wasn't all about getting into dodgy European clubs and dive bars. Time off the boat could more usefully be spent training up. I attended a navigator's yeoman course at HMS *Mercury* in deepest Hampshire, near the quaint old market town of Petersfield, where I learnt all manner of techniques to plot courses on charts and work out the positional movements of the submarine, as well as studying tidal drifts and a host of methodologies with maps, charts and electronic aids. It was an interesting week away, and I was pleased as punch when I was presented with my badge of a gold sextant on a dark navy background, which I wore over my right sleeve.

I also undertook a ship's diving course, spending four weeks in Portsmouth. It was pretty full-on, but I was paid extra every month, on top of my submarine pay, which all helped. I left the service with thousands in the bank, which I later enjoyed spending at university in London. The course was a natural fit for a submariner used to confined spaces and breathing apparatus, and the cold, black waters of the south coast appealed to me from the outset. I did around 40 to 50 dives during the course, with a night dive in the first week, another four night dives over the following two weeks, and then some deeper diving in the final week, as well as learning how to search for explosives on the hulls of ships and techniques for moving up and down on jackstays – a nautical word for ropes – to carry out maintenance. I passed the course and had the ship's divers emblem added to my uniform – an old deep-sea diver's helmet in gold against the dark navy. I was fast becoming a collector of badges, like being in the cubs all over again. All I had to do to maintain qualification was two hours of dives every four months if I wasn't at sea.

Other excursions took me on a variety of journeys. Four of us accompanied an RAF crew flying out of Moray, north-east Scotland. Their main job was to hunt for Russian submarines in the North Atlantic with long-range patrolling that could take them as far east as the Arctic Soviet Union, and west to Greenland and the eastern seaboard of Canada. Shortly after take-off from RAF Kinloss we found ourselves on our way to the oilfields north of Shetland, where the pilot decided to do his own version of angles and dangles. The plane was tossed this way and that as it hurtled along no more than 200 feet above the ocean, banking heavily left and right and then suddenly increasing height; it was time to reach for the sick bags, all of us puking with the excessive movements at speed. Nor did it help that we were so close to the sea – at any point I was expecting us to plunge head-first into the ocean, never to be seen again.

Since being on a submarine is very much a team environment, it was great to get away and do something that involved just myself. Mountaineering in the highlands of Scotland, usually the Cairngorms – its immense views over desolate landscapes of sub-Arctic tundra were breathtaking – was the answer. I loved sucking the cold air of the heights down into my lungs – it made me feel alive and helped me to concentrate, essential as a submariner. It was also a great way to appreciate nature, something I hadn't really considered much before. I'd see mountain hares, ptarmigan and red squirrels, and golden eagles sweeping languidly over the endless mountain ridges, hunting for prey. It was pretty much me against the elements, and I found this return to self-reliance both refreshing and inspiring.

My other pastime was golf. Again, not a team sport – you're on your own, and nothing and no one can help you. You've got a club and that's it to help propel the ball forward. If you're good at it, you get all the plaudits – if you're shit, well, you get the credit for that as well. Long before the likes of Jack Nicholson or Joe Pesci made golf cool, it was the stuffy Colonel Mustard club mentality that kept it in the dark ages.

The antithesis to this was golf in Scotland. On off crew I went out either with two or three crewmates or my brother, and we would play the most famous courses in the world simply by paying the green fees. None of that bollocks about 'you're only playing on a Tuesday in the dark if you were introduced by the club secretary and played lawn tennis with the club captain when you were both in your final year at St Whatnot's'. None of that. We played Troon, St Andrews, Muirfield and Turnberry just by turning up and paying. Fantastic – municipal sport at its best.

Both of these pastimes – on the heights and on the links – felt like marking time, however, for no matter how much fun I was having it was constantly nagging away at me that days like this would soon be over. Like patrol, they were crossed off one by one as the inevitable countdown began, and I knew I'd soon be back below the oceans, away from the world, doing the job I'd volunteered to do and indeed sacrificed my life for from the age of 18.

I believe I played an important if minor part in keeping my country and its population safe from the very real threat of the Cold War. This certainly went unnoticed by the vast majority of the population and doubtless still does today, but the sacrifices that all submariners past and present have made to maintain the safety of the nation have been shrouded in secrecy for far too long. It was the most demanding job I've ever done, both physically and mentally, but striving to be the best team in the whole of the service got everyone through it and motivated us. It was a real pleasure to have served with some of the most knowledge-able and brightest people in the Royal Navy, but it was the boat that kept us all safe from the depths of the oceans and the many dangers that beset me and my fellow crewmates over the years. She let us live inside her and develop together as a team as we moved silently through the ocean without fanfare and bravado, stoically nurturing us and the rest of the crews that served in her.

HMS *Resolution* now lies abandoned in the nuclear graveyard in Rosyth, Scotland, together with her fellow heroes of the Cold War, *Renown*, *Revenge* and *Repulse*, these former giants of the deep all side by side in dock. Britain's first nuclear-powered submarine, HMS *Dreadnought*, has been laid up there since 1980. Once relied upon by both politicians and public alike to keep the country safe, these leviathans sit rotting away, slowly being devoured by the ravages of time, while the politicians decide what to do with them.

I loved my time as a submariner, and I was fortunate that it coincided with the service at its zenith – 33 submarines in total, over three times the total number of working submarines operating today. I could drink, have an occasional smoke if I wished, and we submariners could laugh at each other and at our situation. The buzz I got while serving underwater eclipsed all the negatives, for I was a member of an exclusive club brought together by adversity in a cramped, sometimes boring and very stressful living environment, but to me it was everything and saved me from a life of predictability. Perverse as it may sound, the hardship was all part of the joy. I spent five years in the service, and if I could I'd go back tomorrow and do it all again without hesitation, pot belly and age aside. Life should be full of adventures, and there is none better than being a submariner.

But a different countdown began for me, that of a life outside the world of submarines. I thought it was the right time to leave after my five years, time to move on to new horizons, university and London, loves lost and found, children, books, Claire and peace.

ACKNOWLEDGEMENTS

First, I'd like to thank my publisher, Jack Fogg, whose advice was always spot on and occasionally hilarious, and whose initial brilliant ideas got the ball rolling in the early days of the writing process. Also, the team at HarperCollins for all their hard work. In particular Sarah Hammond, project editor, who has had to put up with enough military acronyms to last two lifetimes. Big thanks as well to Josie Turner, my publicist, marketing guru Jasmine Gordon, art director Claire Ward, audio editorial director Fionnuala Barrett and to Tom Hughes for the illustrations. Also the sales team, Anna Derkacz, Tom Dunstan and Alice Gomer. I'd also like to thank Mark Bolland, Richard Waters and Holly Kyte for their invaluable assistance and James Jinks for his ideas and for checking all things technical. Thanks to my partners in crime at Waterstones, in particular Clement Knox, Bea Carvalho and Peter Saxton.

A big-up to all members, past and present, of the Royal Navy Submarine Service and to submariners of all nations, both new and old, whose self-sacrifice never ceases to amaze me.

Extra-special thanks and big love to my family who have to put up with a bearded, grouchy and, at times, exhausted, ghostly figure over the last 15 months or so. To my children: Isabella, Richard, Betsy and Henry. And a big thank-you to my mum Sheila and brother Chris.

But most of all, thanks to my wife Claire for showing patience and understanding, and dealing with my absurdities on a daily basis.